Take Your Best Shot

Take Your Best Shot

Take Your Best Shot

Turning Situations
Into Opportunities

by Ken Futch

WAGRUB
PRESS

Wagrub Press
Atlanta, GA

Jacket Design - Barry Littmann
Book Interior - Leslie Rains
Editor - Michael Carr
Author Photographer - Tom Wallace

Library of Congress Control No. 2004116000
ISBN No. 0-9763430-0-2

Printed in the United States of America

It's not what you look at that matters,
it's what you see.

—Henry David Thoreau

Contents

Contents

Contents

Chapter Eleven (continued)

Dedication

T his book is lovingly dedicated to Elizabeth C. Futch. She was truly an extraordinary person who served as a role model for our family and our community. Her leadership through service, unconditional love, and encouragement gave me the inspiration to seek greater challenges, the strength to overcome obstacles, and the willingness to share my experiences with others. Thank you, Mother!

Introduction

———————————•———————————

It has always been fascinating to me how people can look at the same situation and see it so differently. Admittedly, I have always seen more humor in tough situations than have most of my friends. Not that they don't enjoy a laugh, but they often need a middleman to point out the humor. There is something funny to be found in nearly every situation; however, some people recognize it more readily than others. Jerry Seinfeld, a master at observational humor, takes routine experiences that nearly everyone can identify with and presents them in a funny light. His audiences have seen those very situations, but missed seeing the humor.

This same concept can be applied to recognizing opportunities. Looking at the same situation, one person may see an opportunity while another may miss it completely. Like humor, there is opportunity in nearly every situation. While no one can spot them every time, we all can improve our numbers by reframing our perspectives.

Having accidentally shot myself in the head and finding even that experience to be loaded with both humor and opportunity helps illustrate my point. I believe that if you can find a positive in accidentally shooting yourself in the head, then nearly any situation in life must be fair game.

Based on my observations, we all regularly encounter situations in our lives ripe with opportunity and will continue to do so as long as we live. This book is about how to recognize and capitalize on more of these opportunities.

Many opportunities cannot be accurately predicted, nor can we necessarily be prepared to handle them all. However, certain proven methods, traits, and behaviors can be determining factors in how we respond. Those who choose to do so can prepare themselves to be in the most advantageous position when opportunity strikes.

To illustrate my points, I draw heavily from my own experiences. I use stories from growing up in a small southern town, navigating the perilous jungles of Vietnam, climbing the corporate ladder (also perilous at times), and building my own consulting and speaking company. I have drawn heavily on my military experience because for me the stress of war somehow made the learning points more dramatic and memorable.

In addition to my personal experiences, I have included several of my favorite fictional humorous stories, which I have placed in shaded boxes.

My goal in writing this book is to help you, the reader, transform more of your situational opportunities into success by being prepared to *take your best shot*.

—Ken Futch

Chapter One

Recognizing Opportunity

———————————•———————————

No great man ever complains for want of opportunity.
—Ralph Waldo Emerson

What if everyone had opportunities for greater success in their lives, but some were blind to them? Success depends on recognizing those opportunities and being willing and ready to take advantage of them as they present themselves.

Some of life's greatest opportunities are heavily disguised. Ironically, sometimes seemingly terrible situations can be found, on reflection, to be major opportunities for success. By honing our recognition and response skills, we open up worlds of opportunities.

From Tragedy to Destiny

A turning point in my life came out of what appeared, on the surface, to be a tragedy. It was an ordinary Saturday afternoon in 1976. Sitting on the edge of my bed talking to my wife Linda, I reached over to the nightstand for no particular reason

———————————•———————————

and picked up my little Saturday-night special, which I kept there in case of a burglary. Noticing that I had picked up the small pistol with the barrel pointing directly toward my face, Linda cried out, "Are you sure the safety is on that gun?"

> I had always heard that right before you die, your life flashes before your eyes. I was sort of looking forward to that, because there were a couple of things I would like to catch again.

Hearing her words, I twisted in her direction and heard a loud boom. The gun had gone off, yet I felt no impact. However, since it had been pointed toward my face, I had the sneaking suspicion that I just might be in some kind of trouble.

I had heard of people cutting off an arm with a buzz saw and never feeling a thing. Throwing the gun aside, I jumped up and raced to the mirror to check for damage. The color drained from my face as I stared at a small hole in my right cheek. When I spotted another hole in my left temple, I *knew* I was dead.

I had always heard that right before you die, your life flashes before your eyes. I was sort of looking forward to that, because there were a couple of things I wanted to catch again.

Blood began to flow out of my nose and mouth as if someone had turned on a faucet. I realized if I didn't die from the blast, surely I would bleed to death; a tourniquet around my neck would not be a great idea! Seeing the blood, Linda ran screaming for the phone to dial 911.

Sensing the end, I sat down on the bed to pray, getting blood everywhere. I knew I did not have time for a long prayer, but I knew I needed to pray. I asked the Lord to please be with me because I was in a real bind this time.

My mind reeled. *Had I really shot myself?* Jumping up, I sped to the bathroom to look in another mirror. I hoped to see things from a new perspective, but nothing had changed. Linda quickly joined me, handing me a towel to catch the blood.

If I don't die, I thought, *there's no need to drip blood all over our new house. I may as well go outside and bleed in the yard.* While Linda stayed behind a few minutes to clean up the blood before it set, I pressed the towel to my face, hurried downstairs, and sat in the middle of the driveway to wait. Listening for the ambulance, I suddenly remembered I didn't have my Blue Cross–Blue Shield card with me. Knowing I would need it, I hurried back upstairs to retrieve that all-important piece of plastic then double-timed it back down to the driveway to wait for help.

After a few more minutes, I heard a siren. A wave of relief flooded me as I envisioned being helped into the ambulance by skilled hands. But instead, a deputy sheriff showed up. That got me thinking. *If I die, they might investigate my wife for my murder, or they might call it suicide, which would horrify my mother.* I decided to take the deputy upstairs, show him the gun, and explain what had happened. Once he was satisfied, I rushed back down to the driveway to continue waiting for the ambulance. Breathing rapidly I thought, *This running up and down the stairs, bleeding like this, is probably not a very good idea.*

The siren had attracted a large number of neighbors, most of whom I did not know, but who were now gathering around me.

"It looks like he broke his jaw," an observer shared with the group.

I thought, *I'll settle for a broken jaw.*

"He needs to lie down," another muttered, as if I wasn't there.

I knew it was not a good idea; I was having enough trouble

with blood running down my throat. One man knelt down beside me, "He must be in shock." Bracing my shoulders, he said, "C'mon now, let's get you down."

Before I could resist, several other people were trying to help my Good Samaritan neighbor grapple me to the ground as I struggled against them.

"Wait!" I said, shaking them off. "I need to sit up so I won't drown in the blood."

The neighborhood "lifesaving" procedures came to an end with the approaching ambulance. The moment the paramedics started an IV, I felt better, just knowing I had something flowing in as well as flowing out. All I could think about was, *Get me to a hospital, put me to sleep, go to work on me, and let me wake up in a room with flowers and cards and guests.* I desperately wanted out of this humiliating predicament.

Linda joined me in the ambulance as we headed for the hospital. Backing up to the emergency room door, two technicians looked in, shook their heads, and immediately began to disagree.

"We can't take him in here; we don't have a neurosurgeon!"

"We should take him in anyway."

Great! I thought, *They're going to argue about it while I bleed to death!*

Finally, they decided to take me inside, where people crowded around me asking, "How did you do it?" I ignored them. It was too humiliating to explain that I had accidentally shot myself in the head. After nearly an hour wiling away precious moments spitting blood into my towel, a doctor examined me briefly and said to the staff, "We can't handle him here. Take him down to Atlanta West and have them alert a neurosurgeon."

I was packaged back up, and away we went in the ambulance to yet another hospital. When we arrived, I immediately felt in better hands. They gave me a little cup to spit in, put some gauze on my face, and soon an orderly bounded in saying, "We need to take you down for X-rays."

Yes! I thought, *Now, we're getting somewhere.*

"Mrs. Futch, we'll have him back in awhile."

Once there, they transferred me to the table and X-rays began. "Hold your head this way. Now this way. Now this way." Then the technician said, "Please stand up and move over here so we can get a chest X-ray."

Startled, I replied, "Look, I'll do anything you folks ask, but my chest is fine. It's my head that has the problem."

"Mr. Futch," the authoritative voice rang, "We always take a chest X-ray of everyone."

I looked at him for a moment and sighed, "Fine." I stepped up, got my chest X-ray, then crawled back up on the stretcher.

When the orderly rolled me back down to the emergency room, a doctor appeared and asked, "Have you had a tetanus shot recently?"

"No," *You've got to be kidding,* I thought. *This is your primary concern!*

Without delay, the doctor plunged the needle into my arm and immediately headed for the door.

I said to his retreating back, "Doc, what's the plan . . ."

He never slowed down.

The X-rays finally arrived. A technician placed them on a wall-mounted viewing box in my cubicle and left. Doctors, nurses, and technicians passed by, but no one stopped to look at them. Frustrated, I finally yelled out, "Can anyone read these things?" Everyone ignored me.

At last, the first doctor returned, looked at the X-rays, and said, "Cancel the neurosurgeon, call an ENT (ear, nose, and throat specialist), and take him to the room."

I liked the part about canceling the neurosurgeon, but what were they planning to do to me in the room he had referred to? With Linda following along, they wheeled me out of the emergency room, put me in an elevator, and took me to an ordinary-looking patient room.

In came an elderly woman dressed in white, carrying a clipboard. I assumed she was a nurse.

"When was the last time you were in a hospital, and where?"

I thought a moment and replied, "Nineteen fifty-eight, in the Pender Memorial."

"Spell that, please."

"P-e-n-d-e-r."

After a moment she said, "Yes, go ahead."

I stared at her, refusing to spell "Memorial." She worked in a hospital; she should know how to spell it.

"All right, what type of pain are you experiencing?"

I realized my head did not hurt all that much, and replied, "Soreness."

"What?"

"Soreness: S-O-R-E-N-E-S-S."

She glared at me, then looked at her clipboard and back at me, "I thought your name was Futch."

Oh, my gracious, I thought. *Is she* on *something?* I looked at my wife and rolled my eyes.

The woman cleared her throat and continued, "Do you sleep with one pillow or two?"

"Two!" I answered crisply.

"Do you take a tub bath or do you take a shower?"

"Shower!" I boomed.

She paused for a moment, "Do you have a problem hearing?"

"Not before that gun went off!"

"Do you have any problem sleeping at night?"

"I didn't last night, but I don't know about tonight!"

Rattled, she looked down at her clipboard to find the next questions. "Do you . . ."

I raised my hand. "Enough!" *I'm worried about lifesaving procedures and she's concerned with room arrangements.* "Are you a nurse?"

"No."

"Are you going to help me?"

"Well, we have routine paperwork . . ."

When I began to laugh, her face went from pink to scarlet. Clutching her clipboard to her chest, she stomped out.

Left alone at last, Linda and I spent the time waiting for the ENT by talking about my insane accident. Happy to still be alive, I wondered what repair procedures the doctor would perform and how painful they might be. The flow of blood into my mouth had slowed, but I still needed my little cup.

The afternoon dragged into evening and still no doctor. When what appeared to be a small bone chip seeped into my mouth, I thought, *Oh, my God, my head may be getting ready to implode! When are they going to do something for me?*

The ENT finally showed up the following afternoon. He came in, looked me over, and said, "You're a very lucky man. It appears the bullet entered your face and went through your nose and sinus cavities. It bypassed your optic nerves and your facial nerve, and then went back out through the side of your head, sort of through a hollow area."

I wish my wife had not heard the "hollow" comment, because she has never let me live it down.

"Don't I need some plastic surgery?"

"No, you'll heal naturally. Bullet wounds are often very sterile injuries. All we frequently do is take a rod, go through the wound, and clean out the debris."

"Not through my head, you aren't!"

Laughing, the doctor said, "Do you have any other questions?"

"Yes. When can I go back to work?"

"Tomorrow. There's nothing really wrong with you."

"But I feel as weak as can be."

"That's just stress, Mr. Futch." Turning to the nurse, he said, "Take that gauze off his face and replace it with two Band-Aids, then process his release."

With no more treatment than a tetanus shot and two Band-Aids, I was on my way home. The *Atlanta Journal-Constitution* found out about my accident and ran a long article. After that, the Associated Press picked up the story and took it nationwide.

I even received a call from *Star* magazine, one of those tabloids that carry stories about women giving birth to alien children. The reporter called me, asking for an interview and a copy of my X-ray.

A little confused about the X-ray, I asked, "Won't it be difficult to read in newsprint?"

He simply said, "We want to put the X-ray in the paper."

"Fine, I'll get it."

When the Star reporter came to my house, he immediately asked for the X-ray. Studying it he asked, "Where did the bullet go through?"

I had known he would not be able to read it. Pointing to the X-ray, I replied, "It went in here and came out there."

He turned to my wife, "Do you have any card paper?" She located some paper, and he used scissors to trim off a narrow strip. Taping the strip to the back of the X-ray, he placed it in front of a lamp and took a picture. The outline of the strip revealed an awesome-looking route through my head.

The story ran in the same edition with a major feature about Farrah Fawcett and TV's *Charlie's Angels*. The "Angels" were on the front page, and I was on the next with a big caption entitled, MAN SHOOTS HIMSELF THROUGH HEAD AND LIVES. My story was put in the proper perspective by another article directly beneath mine entitled: HEN LAYS EGGS THAT ARE BLUE. They had certainly put the freaks on the same page. My friends wanted me to go on the TV show called *That's Incredible*, a 70s reality show where unusual events were reenacted. I told them no way, because I was afraid they would want me to do it again!

As I pondered this near catastrophe in my life, it made me understand the importance of how I spend my time and conduct my relations with other people. I had previously thought, since I had survived the jungles of Southeast Asia and had returned to civilian life, I would probably live out the expected "average" number of years.

Through this incident I realized there was no such thing as an "average" number of years. No one really knows how much time he or she has left. As a result, it is imperative that we make the most of every day, because one day will be our last.

I realized I had been given one more opportunity to do something more with my life. When we really stop to think about it, each day that we wake up, we have another opportunity to do more with our lives.

A few years after my shooting incident, my son came upstairs one Halloween evening and asked, "Dad, would you come downstairs and help me carve a pumpkin?"

Busy writing I said, "Kenny, I'm sorry, I have to finish this report." As he walked away, I thought to myself, *If this were my last opportunity ever to carve a pumpkin with my son, would I do it?* I yelled, "Hold on a second, Kenny. I think I can help you carve that pumpkin!"

As a result of this brush with death, I felt I had been given a loud wake-up call that motivated me to do much more with my life. Still unsure of my mission in life, I began to search with renewed vigor. It took three years of intense seeking, but in 1979 my efforts were rewarded. I attended a positive-thinking rally at the Fox Theater in Atlanta, which featured Zig Ziglar, Cavett Robert, and Dr. Norman Vincent Peale. As I watched those speakers that day, I immediately knew what I wanted to do—become a professional speaker. For the first time in my life, I was able to clearly visualize the career path I wanted to follow.

It took a shot through the head to open my mind . . .

To be successful as a speaker, it is important to have a meaningful message, delivered in an entertaining fashion. I soon discovered that my unusual shooting story was one that audiences thoroughly enjoyed. In a bizarre twist of fate, through what could have been the darkest (and perhaps the last) day of my life, I found the catalyst that helped launch the speaking career that I love so much.

My accident is an example of how opportunities are often

hidden in ghastly situations. It took a shot through the head to open my mind to many possibilities. How we respond to situations is often more important than what has happened to us. While we may not choose all our experiences, we do get to choose how we respond to them. Our choices, good or bad, will dictate our fate, and have the power to change us from a victim to a victor.

The greatest discovery in our generation
is that human beings, by changing the
inner attitudes of their minds,
can change the outer aspects of their lives.
—William James

Chapter Two

Opportunistic Perspective

---•---

We tend to get what we expect.
—Norman Vincent Peale

Awareness of situational opportunities begins when we internalize the concept that opportunities are plentiful and personally attainable. The first step is to recognize that life has provided everyone with abundant gifts and endless ways to use their talents. Where we place our focus can determine our opportunities. By expecting unlimited opportunities, we ultimately determine our reality.

Lesson at Futch's ESSO

When I was a child, my father taught me a valuable lesson about expectations. It was one of those lessons you never forget, that help shape your mind, mold your character, and direct your steps. Dad was an entrepreneur who owned a busy service station in Burgaw, North Carolina: Futch's ESSO. The station was the early-morning hangout for many Burgaw residents. It was the place where hunters and fishermen gathered before taking to the woods or the water, and where they returned to brag and tell wild stories about the "one that got away."

For me, the service station was the center of the universe. There was nothing in life I wanted more than to work at Futch's ESSO with my dad. The only problem was my size. Dad wouldn't allow me to work there until I was "tall enough to reach the center of the windshield." Back in those days we used to wash windshields with every gas purchase, and Dad insisted that I be able to handle the service part of the job before he would even consider putting me on the payroll. And so I waited, chomping at the bit, year after year. It wasn't until I was thirteen that I finally gained the inches to reach the center of the windshield. That was the year I had my first lesson in trust.

It was a warm summer morning in the middle of June. As Dad and I were opening the station for business, I noticed that one of the cabinets where we stocked oil was completely filled with cans.

"Dad," I said, "who filled up this cabinet?"

"The oil man did, son," he replied.

"When?"

"Yesterday afternoon."

"How many cans did he put in here?"

"I don't know," he said, "but if you're all that curious, why don't you go inside and check the invoice?"

"You mean you didn't see him put the cans in here?"

"No."

"Then how do you know the number of cans on the invoice matches what he added to the cabinet?" I couldn't believe my father could miss something so fundamental to the bottom line.

Dad turned, looking me straight in the eye. "Boy," he said with the hint of a smile, "you're going to have to learn to trust some people in this world. Because if you don't, you'll end up a very miserable individual."

That lesson has been reaffirmed in my life many times over. If, while navigating the tangled streets of life, you're always expecting people to cheat you, then undoubtedly they will oblige you. No doubt you've heard the old adage: "You find what you're looking for." A Swedish proverb makes a similar point, but in a positive light: "Those who wish to sing will always find a song."

> Always expect the best and you'll see that the outcome is spontaneously contained in the expectation.
> —Deepak Chopra

The same expectation applies to how we view our situations and the related opportunities. Have you ever noticed how the same people seem to have so many problems in life? Some people are looking for problems, and they consistently find them. Their expectations of problems become self-fulfilling prophecies. Some seem to be looking for reasons why situations caused them to fail (even though the same situations allowed others to thrive). All too often they find they are correct in their beliefs, and the situations do not bring them positive outcomes.

A young sergeant in my platoon in Vietnam demonstrated one of my favorite examples of a negative perspective. He would get up in the morning, look all around, and say, "You know, I can just feel it. We're all going to get killed today." His comment did nothing to instill confidence in the men. We soon had him transferred to another platoon because, if his vision for the future came true, we did not want to share it with him.

Appreciation Drives Attitude

Because our expectations are often shaped by our past experiences, it is essential to develop a personal perspective that focuses more on our past good fortune than on our occasional misfortunes. Your ability to appreciate your past has a profound impact on your vision of the future. My father used to say to me, "Son, how can you ever expect to appreciate what you don't have, if you don't appreciate what you already have?"

> **If every one of us would take our problems to a pile for even distribution, most of us would be glad to return with just the ones we brought**

The ability to appreciate not only drives your outlook on life, but also positions you for future success.

Much too often we do not appreciate something until we lose it. Then, if we get it back, we soon take it for granted again. It seems to be ingrained in human nature.

It's like the grandmother who was walking with her young grandson on the beach. Suddenly a giant wave swept him right out to sea. She began to wail and pray,

"O Lord, if you return my grandson to me, I'll

- continued -

be the BEST grandmother ever!" Immediately, a wave swept him right back onto the shore. She rushed over to her grandson, took him in her arms, looked at him from head to toe, and then looked up at the sky and said, "He had a hat."

Our potential opportunities lay in our ability to recognize our good fortune in life when it occurs. I think we are all blessed. Obviously, some of us are more blessed than others. But even so, I think back to something my mother taught me when I was a child. "If every one of us would take our problems to a pile for even distribution, most of us would be glad to return with just the ones we brought." I think there is a lot of wisdom in that, as there is in that old adage: "I complained because I had no shoes, until I met a man who had no feet."

A recent study shows that immigrants to the United States have a greater probability of becoming millionaires than do native citizens. Most immigrants enter the United States like children entering a candy store, ecstatic over the multitude of options and possibilities. Many of us who were born in this country, however, tend not to appreciate the things we have or the opportunities that await us at every bend. Sometimes we begin to feel that the system is rigged against us. We become jaded and cynical. Some of us expect absolute fairness in every situation and struggle personally with any deviation from our perception of "fair." There will always be situations that do not meet everyone's expectations of fairness.

Here is an example. My wife Linda was a schoolteacher. One of her requirements of her elementary students was that they clean up the area around their desks at the end of the day. Occasionally, a student would say, "I didn't put this paper here; why do I have to pick it up?"

Linda, knowing that this system was the best method to ensure a tidy room, would say, "Well, because it is our room and we all have to help keep it clean."

"But it's not fair," the eight-year-old would say.

Some people struggle with the concept of fairness all their lives. You see and hear it every day in corporate America: "It's just not fair!" The whine of "It's not my job" is also often related to the issue of fairness. The perception of unfairness comes from the feeling that someone expects more from us than should be required. The danger lies in making unfairness an excuse for personal failure.

Life is not fair for anybody, which makes it fair for everybody.

I love what a former boss of mine used to say: "Life is not fair for anybody, which makes it fair for everybody." There is a certain equity in everyone getting a share of inequity. Since all of us have many things in life to appreciate, we should reflect on and appreciate our own good fortune.

Rather than feeling appreciative, many people focus on the "lucky few" who have special gifts and lament, "It's unfair." This is a limiting perspective that disables them from recognizing and taking advantage of their own opportunities. But looking within and recognizing our own gifts in life allows us to better recognize those opportunities. I believe those "lucky few" earned their luck by taking advantage of the opportunities presented to them. Furthermore, it is my goal to enhance your "luck" by showing you how to recognize and take advantage of the opportunities presented to you.

Is it Luck?

I do believe in luck. One of my favorite lines has always been, "I would rather be lucky than good." Just as with opportunity, everyone gets lucky breaks. However, not everyone recognizes and takes advantage of them. Two people can have an identical experience. One seizes the moment; the other does not. The event could be completely random for both. The one taking advantage of the opportunity may be rightly labeled lucky. Should both be described as lucky, or does luck also require action?

Luck has often been described as "preparation meeting opportunity." This perspective is similar to "you make your own luck." This viewpoint, however, does not address all the reasons for good fortune. At times luck can be completely mysterious and inexplicable. While the cause of a fortuitous event may be utterly independent of the person experiencing it, the person's response is usually a determining factor in the outcome.

Thus, there seem to be two requisites for experiencing luck. First, the individual needs to be aware of the good fortune. And this awareness does appear to be enhanced for those who anticipate finding good fortune in life. "Seek and you shall find" seems to play a pivotal role in this concept.

Second, some action is required from the person seeking to experience luck. This is where the preparation component becomes key. When a great opportunity appears, it is extremely helpful to have already developed talents and skills that may be needed. So yes, you make your own luck—by anticipating good fortune, recognizing good fortune when it comes your way, and being willing and able to

> **If you want more good fortune in life, be looking for your lucky break as you prepare by developing your talents and skills.**

take advantage of the opportunity. Many lucky breaks are missed because of the individual's lack of perception and preparation.

If you want more good fortune in life, be looking for your lucky break as you prepare for it by developing your talents and skills.

> I'm a great believer in luck, and I find
> the harder I work the more I have of it.
> —Thomas Jefferson

My Awakening

Before the U.S. Army and my Vietnam experience, I had coasted most of my life, never really achieving excellence in any area. I was an average student at best, a below-average athlete, and, for a North Carolina country boy, not even a very good hunter. In a small southern town, it was important to excel in something, particularly in one of those last two areas.

My first real win in life was my graduation from Officer Candidate School (OCS). For the first time, I was truly committed to taking my best shot. I set my own goal and made up my mind that no matter the cost in effort, pain, or humiliation, I would pay the price to achieve this success. Why? I felt I was a complete disappointment to my father—not because I was a bad kid, but unlike my sisters, who enjoyed great academic success in high school and college, or my cousin next door, who was a great basketball player and superb hunter, I just never excelled at anything. I had ended up in the Army because of poor grades. As a result, I decided that becoming an officer in the army would be an opportunity for me to prove that I could succeed at something. This was a vitally important decision in my early adult development.

Graduation from OCS, coupled with my Vietnam experience, allowed me to see that in spite of my past failures, I should address new situations as new opportunities for success. I had finally tasted success, and for me it became the sweet nectar of ambition. I acquired a different perspective, one that impelled me to take advantage of the many opportunities available to me.

When I returned to UNC–Chapel Hill as a combat veteran, my new perspective of seeking and capitalizing on new opportunities fueled a whole new set of academic behaviors. I began attending classes regularly, unlike my previous college habits. This proved to be one if the most important changes I made. Also, I approached my classes with a completely different attitude. Rather than maintaining a low profile, as I had previously done, I began to sit in the front row and became interactive with my professors. After my experiences in Vietnam, the professors' power, knowledge, and authority no longer intimidated me. I respected them for their accomplishments in their chosen fields; however, I had found life to be multifaceted, with numerous routes to gaining respect and achieving success. My epiphany had come, and I realized that life was something to attack, to fully engage, rather than passively watch it move along. I was no longer content to have whatever came my way. I decided to create my own way.

My new behaviors generated immediate positive results for me. With the start of my second post-Vietnam semester, I was shocked by a new experience. On the first day of class in an advanced marketing course, the professor called the roll. When he called out my name, he stopped and said, "Mr. Futch, I saw your name on the dean's list. It's an honor having you in my class." I thought, *Wow! This is definitely an experience I can get used to!*

My graduation from the University of North Carolina, and my later corporate success, were the result of establishing definite goals and being consistently willing to take my best shot. I learned that even though I had not yet determined my ultimate career path, I could enjoy, learn, and succeed in the opportunities along my life's journey.

Life isn't about finding yourself.
Life is about creating yourself.
—George Bernard Shaw

Stop Worrying and Start Appreciating

Before I was drafted out of college, I worried a lot about flunking out. I did not study; I just worried, and sure enough, my worries came true. As a thirteen-year-old, I had been thrilled to work at my father's service station. In college my worst fear was that I might have to work at a service station for the rest of my life. That should have provided enough motivation to keep me studying, but it didn't.

Then I went to Vietnam. But before I shipped out, what do you think I did? Yes, I worried—the typical masculine worries of one leaving for a war zone: "What if I lose an arm . . . just kill me.

I'd only be half a man."

An interesting metamorphosis happened while I was in Vietnam. I started thinking about the United States and how great it was, how back home, you could get anything you wanted—like a hamburger. It was ironic. I had a hundred dollars in cash on me, a lot of money in those days, but even a hundred dollars could not buy a hamburger in the jungles of Vietnam. In the United States you do not need a lot of status in life or a lot of money to buy a hamburger any time you want.

As I continued my tour of duty in Vietnam, I began to appreciate lots of things I had always taken for granted. I began to think about how much I had worried about flunking out of college and having to work at a gas station for the rest of my life. And I thought to myself, "What's wrong with working at a gas station?" At least I could take regular baths and sleep in a real bed. Oh, and best of all, I could have a hamburger whenever I wanted. In Vietnam the living conditions were harsh. We averaged twenty days between showers. Big rats often crawled on me at night, causing me more stress than the enemy did. Periodic nocturnal attacks by jungle ants added to my misery. A life spent working at a service station began to look a lot more attractive.

Many nights as I lay on the ground in the jungle, I thought about going home. I began to realize that even if I lost an arm, though I would not like it much, it would still be great just to get home. I prayed that if for some reason the Lord saw fit to allow me to make it out of the jungle alive, in whatever condition, I would be forever appreciative. At that point, even losing a limb was better than not making it out of Vietnam alive.

Of course, once I got home, it was not long before I became like other people and slipped into negative thoughts once again.

I complained when somebody cut me off in traffic or stepped in front of me in line. I began to take life for granted again. However, to this day I still use my experience in Vietnam as a measuring stick for life, to help me keep things in perspective.

Reflect upon your present blessings, of which every man has many;
not on your past misfortunes, of which all men have some.
—Charles Dickens

Learn This or Die

In the Army's basic training, there was one message shouted at us many times every day. I will never forget the drill instructor yelling, "If you do not learn this, you will die in Vietnam!" It was repeated so frequently during nearly every activity that it became a joke to many of us. We would mimic the drill instructors saying, "If your boots don't shine, you will die in Vietnam."

At Infantry Officer Candidate School that message evolved. We were regularly told, "If you do not learn this, you will die in Vietnam, and, because of your stupidity, you will cause forty-two of your men to die along with you!" Though I got tired of hearing it constantly, this message resonated with me. It stayed in the back of my mind, a small voice patiently waiting for those times in life when I might need reminding. And its severity always bothered me—such were the potential consequences of making an error.

When I was on the plane to Vietnam, I was terrified. My

greatest fear was not that I might die, although I was certainly aware of the possibility. My overriding concern was that I had not learned and retained enough information to lead my men in combat. I was absolutely horrified at the possibility of making a stupid mistake that would cause someone to die. The responsibility for my forty-two men was not something I could take lightly. It was a serious burden. Finally, I had something that was worth worrying about.

After returning from Vietnam, I was thankful, above all else, that no one had died under my command. Certainly, I will not take credit for that good fortune. A close friend of mine, the most qualified and talented lieutenant I knew, was killed in his first month in Vietnam. I understood the randomness of bullets. A favorite saying of mine at the time was, "I am not worried about a bullet with my name on it, but rather one that says, 'To whom it may concern.'"

One of the greatest tragedies in life is to have an experience and miss the meaning.

I would never recommend combat as a learning tool for anyone, because the risks are too great. I readily admit, however, that I am a better person because of my experiences in Vietnam. Knowing the pain endured by so many, I will always be grateful for my good fortune.

Like many survivors of difficult situations, I often ponder the question: *Why? Why did I make it?* While the answer is impossible to know, the question can be a constant reminder to take advantage of the new lease on life that has been granted.

To develop a positive perspective, we must have something to feel positive about. It isn't something you can fake. Instructing others to develop a positive attitude is like telling someone to laugh. To stimulate laughter, there has to be something funny. Simply asking for laughter is not enough. Likewise, for a person to have a positive attitude, there has to be a reason. While reasons will vary from one person to the next, the stimulus that is available to the masses can be found in appreciating our lives, whatever our current circumstances happen to be.

One of my favorite stories comes from a rabbi who told his congregation, "You should never complain, because God may hear you and He may say, 'You call that bad? Let me show you bad!' You should always say things are good, because then God may hear you and say, 'You call that good? Let me show you good!'"

Sincerely believing in your good fortune, even if that good fortune came through the survival of suffering, can generate an attitude of optimism. One of the greatest tragedies in life is to have an experience and miss the meaning. Whether a painful or a pleasurable situation, the past can help to educate us and position us for today's and tomorrow's opportunities.

We tend to forget that happiness doesn't come as a result
of getting something we don't have, but rather of
recognizing and appreciating what we do have.
—Frederick Koenig

Chapter Three

Responding to Opportunity

———————————•———————————

Opportunity is missed by most people because
it is dressed in overalls and looks like work.
—Thomas Edison

No one lacks for opportunities in life, but many people lack
the ability to recognize and respond to situations as they occur. In
order to awaken and hone this ability, it's helpful to recognize
that opportunities come in two sizes: minor and major.

To succeed with the opportunities that come our way, we must
first understand the expectations and then choose actions that
will exceed the basic requirements for meeting those expectations.
This free-choice decision to willingly exceed the required behav-
ior, whether in a major or minor opportunity, is what I term tak-
ing your best shot.

The Ones That Get Away

Minor opportunities are plentiful; they come at us every day
in our careers and our lives. The major opportunities occur

———————————•———————————

much less frequently, but are usually easier to recognize: a final exam in school, an interview for a job, a key sales presentation. These are the situations where we can see the payoff—the potential benefits are obviously important to our future success. Too often, though, we ignore the minor opportunities because we don't notice them. Minor opportunities are embedded in the most mundane activities: how we answer the phone, conduct ourselves in basic meetings, or write e-mails.

While the list of minor opportunities is endless and covers most common activities, tasks, and encounters, the potential benefits are much less obvious. This lack of perceived value prevents many people from recognizing the opportunity. But the benefits are very real. Minor opportunities allow us to develop the skills and habits that may create major opportunities, and they can also showcase our talents, which may lead to our selection for future major opportunities.

What we miss is the correlation between daily tasks and their inherent opportunities.

Just being aware of minor opportunities prepares us for the major ones, even before the major ones arise. Athletes understand that practice sessions (minor) prepare them for conference games (major). Most people who are not athletes, though, do not find their lives so simply defined in terms of practices and games. Too many of us see only a collection of routine activities punctuated by the rare major event. What we miss is the correlation between the daily tasks and their inherent opportunities. Being unable to identify the minor opportunities, we squander far too many of them. But they are there, embedded within the routine activities that occupy our days. And yet the idea of a business meeting or a memo being a minor opportunity in disguise may seem foreign.

Aiming for the Extras

Every job carries certain expectations. There are daily tasks to be done, most of which we see as routine requirements. Usually someone else, such as a boss, determines these requirements. Many times the expectations are clearly laid out in a written job description. These behaviors could be labeled "required," because once an employee accepts a job, she or he is expected to perform these activities up to a certain standard.

Any behaviors that are *not* required could be labeled "optional." These optional behaviors might be either additional activities or a higher quality of performance in a required task. While meeting the minimum expectation is sufficient for most of these activities, it is going beyond the required that provides the opportunity. Selecting almost any task and choosing voluntarily to excel in it is the starting point to maximizing opportunities. For example, you could decide to make a special effort to energize the way you answer the phone, to improve the traditional memo, or to become more vocal in meetings.

After taking this approach and seizing the minor situational opportunities found in our daily activities, we can then analyze the results: Was it noticed? Did it matter to anyone? Was it fun? Was it even worth the effort? This approach to success can be very low-risk since it is all voluntary. No one even has to know of your plan. You get to choose exactly which activity you want to work on and the degree of effort you want to expend. This low-risk approach offers the opportunity to turn previously routine tasks into new challenges for your personal enjoyment, possible enrichment, and future success.

As I mentioned earlier, learning to identify opportunities is a key ingredient in using daily occurrences to your advantage. These minor opportunities are hidden in your calendar of daily meetings and on your "to do" lists. What makes these activities opportunities is that you, not your boss, can decide where to begin your personal development. The activity you choose for improvement may be something as simple as being more positive in routine meetings or volunteering for a leadership role in a team assignment. Such actions can begin to change or shape others' perceptions of your performance. Another benefit of this approach is that risk of failure is minimal, while the upside can be significant. You get to decide which opportunities you want to pursue, which to encourage others to pursue, and which to skip. The key is to begin to view that next memo you have to write or the next meeting you have to attend, not as just another chore, but as a potential opportunity.

Taking My Best Shot

As an instructor at AT&T's National Sales School, I often worked late in the evenings and on weekends preparing my presentations. Two separate after-hours encounters stand out in my mind as minor situational opportunities. Late one night I ventured down to the cafeteria to get a snack from the vending machine. The only other person in the building was a janitorial worker. He approached me, saying that he had seen me in the building after hours a lot and wanted to know if I got paid overtime for all those hours. I laughed and told him no.

"Then why do you work so much?"

I simply replied, "Because I don't like being embarrassed."

There was an abundance of new material that I had to learn and integrate before I could feel comfortable with my presentations. The fear of looking incompetent to a class was plenty of motivation for me to put in the extra effort—my personal standards exceeded those of the job. Many probably considered this additional work unnecessary.

The other, even more important encounter took place on a Sunday afternoon. I was to give a major presentation the next day, so I went to the school to rehearse. While I was practicing, Joe Rudolph, the National Sales School Director, came into the auditorium to pick up some papers.

"Hi, Ken. I'm surprised to see you practicing. The last time I saw you deliver this presentation, it was really good."

"Thanks."

Not satisfied, he continued. "So why do you feel the need to practice?"

"Joe, practice *is* the reason my past presentations went well."

This mundane activity of practicing for a major presentation is a perfect example of how a minor opportunity can lead to unexpected rewards. Shortly after my chance encounter with Joe, *Newsweek* magazine informed the school about a planned article on our new sales approach and wanted to observe one of our instructors. Although I never found out why I was selected over the other talented instructors, I firmly believed that being seen practicing my presentation on that Sunday afternoon made all the difference.

In trying to maximize opportunities, I rehearsed more than the other instructors. The extra work not only enhanced my skills, I also benefited when others acknowledged my efforts. I am sure that some thought me a fool, while others rewarded me with greater opportunities. Without knowing it at the time, I created a huge opportunity because I voluntarily took it upon myself to practice many optional, minor opportunities.

Turning opportunity into success requires recognizing that every job includes many tasks that could be done differently and perhaps better. Choosing a task and giving it your best shot can be the start of great rewards.

The greatest secret of success in life is for a person
to be ready when their opportunity comes.
—Benjamin Disraeli

Chapter Four

Opportunity Selection

Destiny is not a matter of chance; it's a matter of choice.
It is not a thing to be waited for; it is a thing to be achieved.
—William Jennings Bryan

No one can maximize every opportunity in life—it is not realistic. Indeed, trying to do so can result in more negatives than positives, and make one appear self-centered and greedy. The "choose your battles" approach, so common in parenting advice, applies equally to life's other opportunities.

We should not try to compete in every race; even Tiger Woods doesn't show up for every golf tournament. Every opportunity should be identified, but not all should be pursued. There should be a strategy that includes such variables as risk versus reward, and the probability of success.

Choosing Which Race to Run

In high school, all of our football practices would conclude with wind sprints, where all the players lined up and raced for about

---

twenty yards, then turned around, lined up, and raced back. These wind sprints would last for about ten to fifteen minutes, then the coach would say, "The one who finishes first gets to head for the showers." This winner got to quit for the day and take his shower. The rest of the team would continue, with each winner of the subsequent race heading for the showers. Knowing this was the daily plan, I would save my energy until I heard the coach make this offer. In the next race, even though I had saved my energy, I knew there were a couple of players I could never beat. However, immediately upon their leaving the field, I would always win the next race and head for the showers.

While holding back in the preliminary races may not have helped my stamina—which obviously was the purpose for the exercise—it is an example of assessing situations and choosing when you want to take your best shot. I chose a strategy that worked for me. While I am sure that my coach would not have liked my plan, it got me to my objective, which was to get off the practice field as soon as I could. This example is not an illustration of how to choose worthwhile objectives, or even how to improve your skills. Indeed, my strategy may provide a clue to why I did not excel on the gridiron. It does, however, serve as a case in point for assessing opportunities, having a strategy, and executing a plan.

Doing your best does not mean that you have to exert the maximum amount of energy in every activity. Success is more about awareness and choices.

Recognizing the "Money Shots"

There are those moments in life when we get an opportunity to create what Hollywood calls the "money shot." A motion picture will last approximately ninety minutes, but what audiences will remember and discuss is usually only a couple of minutes or less. For instance, the "money shot" in the movie *Dirty Harry* was "You've got to ask yourself, 'Do I feel lucky?'" In *When Harry Met Sally,* it's "I'll have what she's having." Or in *Crocodile Dundee,* "That's no knife; now, that's a knife!" Anyone who ever saw those

> **Opportunity can appear suddenly and can vanish just as fast, so you must be prepared when your moment arrives.**

movies easily remembers the lines. Directors are always looking for the "money shot." They shoot a lot more footage than they keep, fully aware that not every shot will make the cut. But that eye for the "money shot"—that is, an awareness of what has the greatest opportunity for success—is key to the film's success.

Opportunity can appear suddenly and can vanish just as fast, so you must be prepared when your moment arrives. The magical moments usually come as result of hard work, talent, and opportunity. Too many people merely wait for the lucky break, without doing the preparation. As a result, when the "money shot" opportunity arrives, they are unable to take their best shot.

You have to recognize an opportunity, and when
you see this opportunity, you foster it in some way.
You use it as a springboard to something
better or something higher.
—Erskine Caldwell

While I was an account executive at AT&T, I spotted what I believed to be a "money shot" opportunity. As a result of deregulation, AT&T perceived a need to refocus its sales strategy by having the sales force specialize in various segments of the industry. The premise was that the salespeople should become experts not only in communications, but also in the specific industries to which they were selling. So anyone selling to carpet manufacturers was to become an expert in the carpet industry, thoroughly understanding it in order to bring an outside consultative expertise to the table.

This program was called "system selling," with a focus on applications that solved the client's business-related problem. The account executive would be positioned with the industry's leaders and thus understand their objectives, operations, and concerns. Based on this understanding, the account executives would lead teams providing in-depth system studies to make recommendations for improvements that would provide a favorable return on investment.

After AT&T had introduced and implemented this program, the next step was to evaluate the effectiveness of its salespeople. A certification program was designed to enforce compliance with the new approach. A new title of account executive–industry consultant (AE-IC) would be given to salespeople who met the new requirements.

All salespeople were given thirty days to develop a portfolio for submission to a panel, proving that they were able to sell applications and that they were viewed as experts in their industry. The areas of focus were specified, but salespeople were not told what would necessarily constitute success in each area. So the challenge for those in my position became one of determining both what the panel of judges would actually be looking for, and how to present our material in a way that would meet with success.

Complaints and frustration in the sales force were at an all-time high. The salespeople considered the process unfair and ridiculous and were anxious about the time spent away from their real jobs. We were told that if we did not pass, we would be notified of the sections we had failed and would be given a chance to resubmit those sections of our portfolios.

Some salespeople decided not to worry too much about the first submissions, to wait and see what was deemed successful, and then resubmit after getting a better understanding of the exact certification requirements.

A peer of mine at the time told me he was not going to work on this project in the evenings or weekends, because in twenty years no one would know whether he ever became certified as an AE-IC, but his family would know whether he spent quality time with them. I agreed one hundred percent with that theory as an overall approach to balancing one's life for long-term success. However, there are those times when one must recognize the short-term window of opportunity and work extra hard to win the prize.

Although this seemed a horrible and time-consuming task, I knew that the company had invested millions in this program and was intent on making it work. I had never enjoyed writing papers in college and certainly did not see this as my strength. While I knew that the requirements for success would be steep, the company would want at least one person to be successful in order to prove that it could be done. I decided that early success might bring me a lot of extra recognition, so I would try to be that person. I believed this was a major opportunity.

I was determined to "put it all on the line" the first time. Never in my life had I put more hours into a project. I averaged fifteen hours every day during this thirty-day period. The portfolio development was similar to creating a thesis. My final submission was a 300-page document.

> **Your success often depends on your ability to choose your races, and on your willingness to commit to whatever is required for success.**

The rewards more than justified my efforts. I was the first one in the company to be certified as an AE-IC and one of only three to succeed on the first submission. The accolades were phenomenal. I was held up as the "poster boy" for the new sales approach. I was asked to speak around the country to other organizations in our company on why this sales approach was chosen and on the related benefits.

Although I also achieved the top sales results in our 6,000-person sales force, the accolades of becoming the first AE-IC overshadowed all my other accomplishments and gave me several opportunities for advancement. I eventually accepted a promotion to a job I had been craving, which was to teach sales skills at the newly created National Sales School, located in Denver, Colorado. This nationwide exposure as an AE-IC catapulted my further success in the company.

We have to recognize that it is impossible to win every race. The key is to recognize which races are the most important. Once you make that determination, do not hold back, but give it your all. Your success often depends on your ability to choose your races, and on your willingness to commit to whatever is required for success.

Life is often compared to a marathon, but I think
it is more like being a sprinter; long stretches of
hard work punctuated by brief moments in which
we are given the opportunity to perform at our best.
—Olympic gold medallist, Michael Johnson

Chapter Five

The Best Shot Requires Knowing a Good Shot

———————————— • ————————————

The greatest obstacle to discovery is not ignorance
—it is the illusion of knowledge.
—Daniel J. Boorstin

Traditionally, taking your best shot has been thought of simply as doing your best. For many this means putting forth the greatest degree of effort possible. To give one's "best shot" certainly includes this traditional aspect of individual effort; however, knowing how the shot will be evaluated is also a worthwhile variable to consider.

It is impossible to take your best shot without knowing what constitutes a good shot. Knowledge and skills must be coupled with effort to achieve real success, and it is this continuous refining of knowledge, skill, and effort that improves individuals and increases their probability of success.

———————————— • ————————————

The Perpetual Student

Achieving success usually requires more than a cursory understanding of the opportunity. In-depth knowledge of a subject can reveal opportunities invisible to the uninitiated.

Many opportunities prove more complex when examined thoroughly. For example, in order to provide excellence in customer service, one must first understand what would make customer service excellent. While most people easily recognize the value of politeness and competence, to insure success it is important to understand the role of customer expectations.

It is impossible to take your best shot without knowing what constitutes a good shot.

Enhanced knowledge positions us to understand the reasons behind potential future decisions, even when those reasons are unknown to the decision maker. For instance, clients of interior designers frequently struggle in articulating their requests. They often say, "I can't explain it, but I know what I like," or "I will know it when I see it." Successful designers understand the variables that influence preference, such as color, lighting, spacing, and so on, and use that knowledge to achieve success.

An enhanced awareness of a subject often teaches us why certain items are important and have greater value. This principle is important in art and music appreciation courses, which teach the concepts and background needed in order to understand and enjoy art and music forms that might otherwise be dismissed.

What others value is not always obvious—even to themselves. Perceptions of our knowledge and professionalism can sometimes be based more on image than on reality. For this reason, our knowledge base should include an understanding of the subtle image factors that influence others' perceptions.

Some factors that many consider superficial can often have a significant impact on how others perceive our capabilities. Early in my career, my company hired an image consultant to improve the dress and appearance of those in the marketing organization. I looked forward to my meeting with the consultant, not worried in the least about my existing attire. In anticipation of the consultant's critique, I decided to wear my best suit. Listening to his feedback, I was utterly shocked. Every item I had on was wrong: my suit, my shoes, my shirt, my tie. The consultant did not say anything about my underwear, but then again, he did not see my underwear. He was very tactful. He did not say to me, "Ken, why don't you just throw all your crap away?" What he did say was, "The next time you purchase a new suit, you might consider conforming to these particular guidelines . . ." So I went out the very next week and bought a new suit, using his recommendations.

Working late one evening two weeks later, while wearing my new suit, I was stopped by the night watchman. This man, with only a third-grade education and certainly not acquainted with John Molloy's book *Dress for Success,* or Susan Bixler's *The Professional Image,* asked a very insightful question: "Mr. Futch," he said, "how do you like your job now that you got that big promotion?"

Since all I had was a new suit, not a promotion, I quickly realized how small changes could make major differences in the way others perceive us. By understanding more of the factors that influence perceptions, we can increase our probability of success. Some people refuse to submit to expectations that they believe to be unimportant—quite often to their own detriment. Certainly no one should violate his or her ethics, or even try to project a false image, just to take advantage of an opportunity. But we should always be aware of how our choices influence our ability to achieve opportunities.

By becoming a perpetual student in search of additional knowledge in your chosen area, you can make your next best shot better than your last best shot. Over time your best shot should become better and better.

The Best Teacher

Many believe that experiential learning is the preferred kind. But learning can happen in many different ways: in classrooms, seminars, books, and in a thousand other ways. My mother used to say, "Experience may be the best teacher, but a fool will learn by no other." Certainly, learning by experience can be priceless, but there is not always time for a lengthy learning curve. Experience is not always the best approach, nor does it work for everyone; however, it often does work when no other method will.

> **Experience may be the best teacher, but a fool will learn by no other.**

I often learned the hard way, through experience rather than instruction. When AT&T transferred me to Denver, I decided to take advantage of the locale and learn to ski. With my water-skiing background, I thought I should be able to transfer that skill quickly to the slopes. I felt that all I needed was a little experience. I opted out of any formal instruction and simply took the lift up the mountain. It was a big mistake. Taking three hours to get down my first run, I soon realized I needed more than my water-skiing experience—I needed someone who knew what they were doing to tell me what I should be doing.

I found a ski instructor, and he took me back up the mountain. When we got off the lift, he said, "Take off and ski a little bit, and let me watch you." It was not a pretty sight.

Quickly catching up to me, he offered several pointers I will always remember. "The first thing you're doing wrong is that you're not properly balanced on your skis."

I thought to myself, *Well, I had an idea of that!*

He continued, "Hold your poles out about chest high, and that will help keep you balanced. The next thing you're doing wrong is that you're looking at your skis. Don't look at your skis; look where you want to go."

At that point I thought, *That would be home.*

"Also, when you turn, you turn too far and start going back uphill, then you come down the hill backwards."

"Yes, that bothers me a lot!"

He then explained, "And, finally, you should always keep your shoulders pointed downhill, because if you do, your body will follow."

Those were just a few suggestions that made a drastic difference in my ability to ski. With that advice, I navigated my second run much more successfully than my first. If I had just kept on trying to learn on my own, I might still be on the mountain somewhere. I will credit myself with knowing, at least in this situation, that experience alone might not be the best method of learning to ski. Incorporating the advice of others can usually shorten the learning curve.

However, not all advice is equal. Some advice can even be harmful. I experienced this personally, also on the Colorado ski slopes.

One Saturday morning, a friend called and said, "Do you want to go spring skiing with us?"

I said, "Sure, what should I wear?"

"Wear your bathing suit." Well, that made me somewhat skeptical, but I put one on. When they came to pick me up, I glanced out the window to see what they were wearing. They all had on shorts or bathing suits. So I felt a little relieved that I was not being misled. We rode to the ski resort, and I got out and looked to see what other people were wearing. Some had on shorts, while most had on regular full ski outfits. I thought, *I guess I'm on the cutting edge.* We rode the lift to the top of the mountain. As we skied off the lift, my friend said, "Ken, be sure you don't fall."

I immediately asked, "What do you mean?"

"At this time of year, daytime temperatures rise, melting the surface of the snow, and it freezes overnight. So in the mornings, it's ice, almost like crushed glass. If you fall on it, it will cut you."

"Now you tell me, after getting me up here like this!" On my first trip down, I lost my balance and fell. However, it was not like one of my normal, spectacular spills, but just a small fall over onto one knee. Nothing hurt, but when I looked down to see if I had done any damage to myself, I realized that the snow had removed a layer of skin off my entire knee. I thought, *Well, it doesn't really hurt, maybe because of the cold. I think I'll continue skiing since I've already paid for a full-day lift ticket.* I then skied to the bottom and got back in line for the lift.

Everyone was staring and pointing, saying, "Look at that man's leg!"

As we rode back up the lift, my friend said, "Ken, you really should go to the first aid clinic."

"What would they do?"

"Put a bandage on it."

"What would that buy me?"

"If you were to fall again, it might protect it."

"Well, if I followed that logic, I would put the bandage on my good knee. This one is already gone!"

We skied the rest of the morning without incident, and then we stopped for lunch. After lunch, I went back up and had one of my regular falls, this time removing a large portion of skin from my elbow. I said, "That's it! I quit!"

I went back to the bottom of the mountain and sat on the deck, waiting for my friends to finish for the day. Every person who came by would say, "Wow, that looks bad!"

Two people said, "Yeah, I saw that at lunch!"

"You did? Well, I got this since lunch!" and showed them my elbow.

The point of this story is that while we should seek advice from multiple sources, we must remember that not all advice is good—and sometimes it's downright harmful. However, by obtaining more information, you have a larger base of advice from which to make a decision. You can always choose to disregard any particular advice. All advice should be filtered, using your own knowledge and experience. Then use your personal judgment before determining a course of action. If I go spring skiing again in the future, I will wear protective covering. You will not see me on the slopes again in a bathing suit.

Seeking minor opportunities to practice certain behaviors can enhance your skill level. However, experience alone is seldom enough. We also need to know whether our aim is improving and whether we are hitting the target. Continuing to take shots without the benefit of feedback from others, and without our own internal assessment of progress, will not lead to a best shot later.

For example, if a kid wanted to join a rifle team and someday go to the Olympics, she could begin to shoot at targets, hundreds of times each day. But, she would not improve unless she walked out periodically and checked to see how often she had hit the targets. Simply practicing an activity will not bring success—we have to assess the result of the practice.

Taking your best shot requires understanding what makes a shot good. As we improve our aim, we are often able to appraise our personal development. The ability to quantitatively measure improvement in personal growth is often extremely rewarding. It is human nature to feel invigorated when you are improving your talents and your abilities. Conversely, stagnation leads to depression. Those who consistently take and make their best shots are the ones who learn and continuously improve the shots they are taking.

> The better I get, the more I realize
> how much better I can get.
> —Martina Navratilova

Chapter Six

Success Ratio Enhancers

———————————————•———————————————

War is ninety percent information.
—Napoleon Bonaparte

*In order to be best prepared to take advantage of new oppor-
tunities, it is often helpful to analyze past situations to determine
which factors have played a role in your success. There are certain variables, characteristics, and tactics that can significantly
improve your chances for success. Recognizing more of these factors and understanding their effect can mean success with your
next opportunity.*

Timing the Moment

The awareness of strategic moments, what some people call
timing, is a combination of preparation and luck. My first
lesson in this also came at Futch's ESSO. A favorite activity of
the men who congregated there was a game called "traveling," a
small gambling pastime. First the men would determine who

would buy cokes for everyone by a series of coin flips. The last remaining person had to purchase the Cokes for the grand price of ten cents apiece. Before the Cokes were dispensed from the machine, each person put a dollar in the pot. Back in the 1960s, the location where the bottle was originally filled was stamped on the bottom. The winner of the pot would be the holder of the Coke that had been bottled at the most distant location. Sometimes maps were consulted to determine the exact distances and the ultimate winner. Occasionally, the bottle was smooth on the bottom, with no city listed. These were considered to be from outer space and were automatic winners.

As a youngster watching this activity, I learned that whenever my father won, his spirits were much improved. I found these occasions the ideal time to make particular requests, such as asking for time off for a special activity. My success rate was greatly enhanced if I approached Dad while he was feeling particularly fortunate. In this way I learned that timing the strategic moment to pursue an opportunity can make a major difference in the outcome of any situation.

Make a Decision, Candidate

Attending the Infantry Officer Candidate School in Fort Benning, Georgia, I was quickly immersed in an environment that emphasized the consequences of decision-making. In this twenty-three-week curriculum, leadership assignments shifted every three days. This rotation was designed to maximize leadership opportunities and to simulate decision-making "under fire." As a result, a candidate might serve as captain one day and as a private the next.

When we drew an officer's role, our tact officer (comparable to a drill sergeant in boot camp) would verbally harass us. While we were trying to give orders to the men, he would stand inches from our faces, screaming questions and comments at us. I can still remember my tact officer shouting, "What are you going to do now, candidate? People are dying, candidate! What are you going to do? Make a decision, candidate!" The tact

> **. . . A slow decision, even if correct, can be as deadly as a bad decision.**

officers justified their harassment by saying, "If you are too stressed and unable to give orders with me yelling in your face, how will you be able to give orders when the enemy is shooting bullets at you?"

Our training emphasized not only making the right decisions, but also making them quickly. We became acutely aware that a slow decision, even if correct, can be as deadly as a bad decision. We often discussed two seemingly contradictory adages for decision-making. The first was "Look before you leap." It is easy to see the logic of this approach, particularly when your next step might be on a booby trap or into an ambush. The other was "He who hesitates is lost." This was appropriate when the shooting began, because pausing to ponder could quickly bring death for an officer and his men.

Both approaches are appropriate at different times and in different situations. Some people take pride in their ability to make quick decisions, while others are smug about the quality of their decisions. But reliance on any single strategy for decision-making is a risky plan. The ability to recognize which strategy to employ is learned through experience by using both approaches.

Many people miss countless opportunities because they are unable to make a decision. They suffer from "paralysis by analysis." Rarely can we wait for all the data to come in. Success often depends on knowing when to make a decision using the available data. The ability to "pull the trigger" is often the prime factor in responding to opportunities.

Intelligence is quickness in seeing things as they are.
—George Santayana

Blessed With Failures

When I was invited to make the commencement speech at my former high school, I was not quite sure what I could say that would have real meaning for the graduates. Then I remembered how the fear of failure prohibits so many people from maximizing their potential. I thought these students could relate to that fear. So I told them that as a child growing up, I was blessed with many failures. I grew accustomed to failure. I believe that these failures made me willing to try new things in life.

I then shared with the graduates the humiliating experience of being on our high school football team, losing 88 to nothing at our homecoming game. What made my humiliation even more demoralizing was that I spent the game warming the bench. I was not as good as our other players. Years later I understood the blessing of this event: I no longer feared failure, for I had been through the worst and had survived.

In August 2003, our team's failures were highlighted in a National Public Radio commentary delivered by my high school friend and classmate Gary Trawick, now a superior court judge:

88 TO NOTHING
by Gary Trawick

Wallace–Rose Hill was the archrival of Burgaw High. I was a sophomore at Burgaw. The year was 1960, and the Red Devils had not won a game in two years. I have never understood why someone would choose Wallace for our homecoming game. It seems to me that homecoming should be a happy occasion, and the prospect of beating the Bulldogs never seemed to make for a happy occasion.

It was a perfect football night. It was in October–just cool enough for the cheerleaders to need to wear the wool athletic jackets of their player boyfriends. There had been the usual homecoming parade, the picking of a homecoming queen, and the planning of the big dance after the game.

Kenneth Futch ran the ESSO service station in Burgaw. He was the father of Kenneth Futch Jr., whom we called Kenny Boy, and who was also a sophomore member of the team. He (Futch Sr.) was also the husband of the high school algebra teacher. He was the most rabid Burgaw Red Devil fan in town. He was a devout Methodist, and while that did not make him the equal of a backslidden Baptist, it did put his operation of the time clock beyond question.

- continued -

Wallace won the toss and elected to receive. The teams lined up, the center placed the ball on the tee, the fans stood for the kickoff, the cheerleaders were hollering and waving their pom-poms in the air, the whistle blew, and the kicker ran to the ball and sent it downfield to the twenty-yard line. About ten seconds later all the referees had their hands pointing to the sky, signaling the first touchdown for Wallace. During the first half this would be repeated eight more times.

The coach did not even come into the locker room at halftime. There was no cheering from the Red Devil side as we left the field. The only cheering came from the Wallace–Rose Hill side, which was a steady and loud chant of–"We want a hundred. We want a hundred. We want a hundred."

The second half is where Kenneth Futch, in spite of his devout Methodism, in total disregard of being the husband of one of the most respected teachers of the high school, putting aside his role model responsibilities to his son, yielded to temptation to help the Red Devils. During the second half of play, he never allowed the clock to stop. It ran after incomplete passes. It ran after Bulldog touchdowns. It even ran during time-outs. When the final whistle blew, the score stood at eighty-eight to nothing. The Bulldogs didn't make a hundred, because the timekeeper was on the side of

- continued -

the Red Devils.

It is easy to think no good can come from such total humiliation. I can without equivocation tell you I learned one of life's most important lessons that night. During my life I have attempted many things that appeared from the beginning to be doomed to failure. Sometimes it was lawsuits in which it appeared I had no chance of winning. It was so the first time I ran for political office, me coming from a little small county and running against a candidate in the big neighboring county. It was true the time I set out to build a sailboat in my back-yard.

People would say, "You can't win. You're going to be humiliated." When I hear these comments, I simply smile and inside say, "You just don't under-stand. When you have lost a homecoming game to your archrival eighty-eight to nothing, life sim-ply cannot hold any humiliation greater than that."

I often tell younger lawyers that I never learned much from the cases I won. It is the cases I lost that taught me the most. My junior and senior years, our team had respectable seasons and won some games. However, the most I learned about life from football came from a score of eighty-eight to nothing.

I learned from playing on this team that while failures may be plentiful and painful, they are not final, and life continues. My devoted family still loved me on the Saturday morning after my team had suffered another embarrassing defeat. I realized that you could move on after a failure and take on other opportunities and succeed. Nobody succeeds at everything they do, and everybody fails at something.

There will always be failures, and there will always be more opportunities for success. The danger lies in allowing our past failures to stymie our future efforts. By viewing failures as an integral part of our success cycle, we can expedite our success and save ourselves countless hours of regret and despair.

There will always be failures . . . The danger lies in allowing our past failures to stymie our future efforts.

It is sometimes possible to overemphasize success. For example, Judge Trawick told me that choosing an attorney who had never lost a case was a bad idea. To him, if the attorney had never lost a case, it meant he would not take difficult cases, or he would get his clients to "cop a plea." He said good attorneys always have a few losses, which help them explore new boundaries.

Dennis Conner captained a losing America's Cup sailboat-racing team for several years. He truly believes in celebrating failures. Before he and his crew won their first America's Cup, he would have the crew increase the speed of the sailboat until something broke. Then they would celebrate whatever it was that had broken. One day they pushed so hard that they broke the mainmast. Rather than getting upset, they opened a bottle of champagne and celebrated. Conner said they now knew exactly how fast they could go. Shortly after this, he and his crew won the America's Cup.

I shared Connor's story with an executive of a company in Orlando, Florida, who had been seeking to instill a creative spirit in his sales and marketing efforts. He immediately decided to institute an award in his organization for the most impressive failure. He wanted everyone to realize that their future success depended on their discovering new sales applications. If only success is rewarded, most people will just do traditional things. However, rewarding unusual but creative efforts—even if they are unsuccessful—encourages others to take calculated risks. Without risk taking, nothing new would be created, nothing spectacular would be invented, and the world would become a stagnant, boring place.

Sometimes opportunities come our way that are exciting and yet scary. I am a member of the National Speakers Association, which holds workshops and a national convention every year. To be selected as the opening keynote speaker is considered a great honor. When I was chosen for this opportunity, I felt very excited, but also a little fearful. Speaking to your peers can be a big challenge. On one hand, they are the most enthusiastic and supportive audience a speaker could address. On the other hand, however, they are internally evaluating every aspect of the presentation with a very critical gauge.

I received almost a year's notice before my speech. This gave me the opportunity to be thoroughly prepared. My friends liked to encourage me with comments like "If you ever mess up a speech, don't let it be this one!" I probably spent more time preparing for this non-paid speech than for any other speech in my life.

I believe in visualizing the results that we desire. The more we hold an image in our minds, either positive or negative, the greater the probability that that image will become reality. So, in addition to preparing for my presentation, I spent many hours visualizing a great audience reaction, followed by wonderful feedback from my friends and from speakers I had not yet met.

The speech took place in Chicago in February, and in spite of the frigid weather, attendance was large. My introducer did a superb job of extolling my virtues and creating anticipation for my presentation. Although in my mental preparation I had tried to think of the most positive reception possible, I could not believe how reality surpassed my wildest dreams. After my speech, accolades flowed all weekend and continued for weeks. It was one of those experiences that I call life's great gifts. Although the pleasure was fleeting, I call up positive memories such as these to serve as my personal motivational fuel for new challenges.

Seldom can one enjoy a mountaintop experience without accepting some level of risk. If you are not willing to take risks, you greatly limit what you can achieve. That itself should be a risk you are not willing to take. With either success or failure, there are growth opportunities. Encountering these experiences teaches us that the highs of success and the lows of failure are both temporary. The willingness to risk often plays a big part in the evolution of potential.

I've missed more than 9,000 shots in my career.
I've lost almost 300 games. Twenty-six times I've been trusted to take the game-winning shot and missed.
I've failed over and over again in my life.
And that is why I succeed.
—Michael Jordan

It's Not About Sex

I can thank my wonderful family for helping me to avoid a common pitfall of discriminating in the workplace. When we were growing up in the 50s, I never imagined that my three sisters (two older, one younger) would play such a large part in helping me deal with the changing roles of women in the business world.

I, for one, was never able to believe that men were inherently smarter than women. My sisters finished at the top of their classes. One sister was the valedictorian of her high school class and went to Duke University on a National Merit scholarship. My other sisters also went to college on scholarships. In contrast, I was just lucky to get into a college.

While I was struggling to stay in the University of North Carolina, my sister (the valedictorian) took the Law School Admission Test and finished in the top one percentile. She received a full scholarship to Yale Law School while I was receiving my Army draft notice from Uncle Sam.

For a number of years my mother held the top academic record at her college. My father, while a very talented man, had only finished high school. So when people would talk to me about equality of the sexes, I was always quick to agree. I liked the idea of being equal to them—bringing me up to their level!

Inadvertently, my family had prepared me well for dealing with the changing times that lay ahead. I did not labor under any false notion that men were intellectually superior to women. By eliminating limiting biases, we create greater opportunities for everyone, starting with ourselves.

Questions Are the Answer

In persuading others to support our action plan, questions can be our best ally. I found out about the persuasive power of questions in 1966. That was the year I held the high honor of being the first student drafted out of the University of North Carolina for the Vietnam War. The people in power must have said, "If you gotta send somebody, send him." I will never forget that day. The letter I received read: "Greetings from the President of the United States of America. You have been selected by your friends and neighbors . . ."

At that point, I wanted to kill my friends and neighbors. I thought about my situation, *Well, since I'm being drafted, I have a two-year obligation. If I were to join, I would have a three-year obligation. Why would anybody in their right mind join the Army and have to spend three years in the military instead of two?* I decided to pose that question to the army recruiters. So, I went to the post office, where the recruiters hung out, and I asked my question. The recruiter was the first skilled salesperson I had ever encountered. He understood the self-discovery technique, which often allows people to determine answers for themselves.

If *you* say it, they doubt it; if *they* say it, they believe it.

He said, "Do you have a date when you're going in (the Army)?"

"Certainly. They've got me. I'm gone."

"What kind of job do you think they'll give you?"

"I don't know. Considering my academic background, I guess some type of clerical position."

"So, are you saying that you think you're a little bit smarter than everybody else, and as a result they're going to give you a good desk job?"

"Well, I wouldn't word it quite that way."

"Well, then, let me ask you another question. Do you think they put all the dumb people in the infantry?"

"I never really thought about that," I answered.

"Then let me ask you another question. Can you see any problem with putting just the dumb people in the infantry?"

I quickly said, "Where is it that I need to sign to guarantee that I become a clerk?" At that point I realized that I was willing to spend another year in the army to guarantee myself a clerical position. (Later, as a result of not fully understanding my opportunity for Officer Candidate School, I ended up in the infantry anyway.)

This recruiter understood the value of asking questions rather than making statements. He never told me what they would do to me; he simply asked questions. My own imagination could conjure up worse images than he could ever have painted for me.

When we are trying to persuade others to our way of thinking, often it is best to ask questions and let them discover the answers for themselves. Keep in mind the old adage: "If *you* say it, they doubt it; if *they* say it, they believe it."

This self-discovery process encourages others to support our efforts, while seeing the wisdom of their own logic. People seldom argue with their own facts.

Quick On the Praise

The ability to be assertive without being perceived as aggressive can generate opportunities. While facilitating a consensus-building exercise in a communication skills class, I began to notice a particular variable that led to a great degree of success.

In an employee-promotion role-playing exercise designed to teach conflict resolution, each participant's objective was to get his or her "candidate" selected for a promotion. This exercise used groups of five participants, with ground rules requiring majority rule, and had a thirty-minute time limit. Each participant was given a sheet with the candidate's background, including work history, experiences, strengths, and weaknesses. Each candidate was qualified for the promotion.

The challenge was to present one's own candidate effectively, listen to the other presenters, and then decide who would get the promotion. The skills involved included presentation skills, listening skills, and the ability to be seen as objective and unbiased. Because everyone had the competing goal of getting their particular candidate selected, quick decisions were seldom reached.

The successful participant, each time I observed this exercise, employed a tactic that I was not teaching. In addition to using effective people skills, the successful participant was the first person in the group to make a positive comment about another's candidate. Being the first to praise a candidate other than one's own seemed to position this individual as one who could rise above selfish motives and recognize the potential in others. This minor acknowledgment of another candidate's attributes was enough to secure at least one other vote from another participant—usually one who had given up on his or her probability of success and had already been offended by someone else's bullying tactics.

There is a fine line between being perceived as simply assertive and being negatively characterized as aggressive. The technique of being first to acknowledge publicly the positive attributes of conflicting positions can sometimes provide the slight edge that enables success.

Firing a Better Shot

Deems Futch, my grandfather, was a large man with big plans. His special talent was recognizing present and future value, particularly in timberland. As a result, he was able to acquire a lot of land in Eastern North Carolina. A side benefit for him was a lot of great places to go hunting. Often he would invite friends and business acquaintances to join him on hunting trips.

He once invited some state politicians and the leading gubernatorial candidate to one of his choice locations for a hunting trip. Since his road was particularly muddy, my grandfather decided to park in the yard of a farmer living next to his property.

At the end of the hunt, as my grandfather and friends returned to his car, the farmer stormed onto the scene with rage in his eyes, obscenely cursing my grandfather for parking on his property. He further threatened my grandfather by yelling, "If you ever park on my land again, you'll have hell to pay!"

Very calmly my grandfather said, "John, you know that hog pen you have behind your house? It's actually on my property. And that garden that you plant each spring—it is also on my land. But let me add, your hog pen and garden don't bother me at all. You go right ahead and continue to use my land as you please."

At that point, my grandfather turned and walked to his car. The farmer quickly followed, apologizing profusely, and said, "Deems, I was a bit hasty in what I said before. Don't you worry about parking in my yard. Feel free to do so any time you please."

I always felt that my grandfather's response was unusual

because it wasn't the easy thing to do. His "better shot" was much more effective than returning the farmer's anger. My grandfather's tactic is one that can heal relationships and avoid unproductive conflicts. While revenge may be sweet for the moment, retribution seldom builds bridges. "Getting even" usually creates additional hurt feelings and further deteriorates relationships.

I have found that people who often say and do the nastiest things have typically spent a lot of time in a negative environment. As a result, they are very familiar with ugly behaviors and are often very skilled at ugly demonstrations. The point to remember is that they usually know "ugly" better than you do, and you can rarely "out-ugly" them. What they do not understand or anticipate is a positive response. The old adage of "kill them with kindness" is still appropriate today. When someone returns politeness in the face of ugliness, it is not a game the "uglies" are used to playing. Being polite in the face of "ugly" can produce positive results.

Showing Your Warts

One of the quickest ways to begin building a relationship with others is to demonstrate your own vulnerability. Sometimes, in a misguided effort to put their best foot forward, people can build a wall of success between themselves and others. When two people meet and they only discuss their successes, the relationship will remain on a superficial level. It is only when one is willing to admit a personal weakness that the relationship can move to a deeper level. This disclosure is a signal to the other person that it is okay to be open and honest, without trying to impress.

A lion who is making his daily rounds in the jungle comes upon a monkey. He says, "WHO is the king of the jungle?"

The monkey says, "Why, you are, Mr. Lion."

The lion slaps him upside the head and says, "Don't you ever forget it!"

He then comes upon a weasel. He says, "WHO is the king of the jungle?"

The weasel says, "Why, you are, Mr. Lion."

The lion then slaps him and says, "Don't you forget it!"

The lion then comes upon an elephant. He says, "WHO is the king of the jungle?"

The elephant stops what he's doing and looks at the lion. Then he takes his trunk, wraps it around the lion, lifts him up, pops him against a tree on the left—BAM!—slams him against a tree on the right—BAM!—then he slings him about seventy-five feet in the air.

The lion hits the ground, jumps up, dusts himself off, looks back at the elephant and says, "If you don't know the answer, just say so!"

People who freely admit that they do not possess all the answers demonstrate both humility and honesty. These are critical bonding traits.

In seeking to connect with others, it is important to remember that people will relate more to our failures than to our successes. Of all the stories told about Michael Jordan, the one I have most enjoyed is the story of his greatest disappointment.

> **... people will relate more to our failures than to our successes.**

Michael Jordan went to Laney High School, which is about twenty miles from my hometown of Burgaw. In 1978, his sophomore year, he tried out for the varsity basketball team, and the coach informed him that he was not talented enough and cut him from the team. (I have always found it humorous that this coach was later chosen to become head coach in Burgaw.)

More people can relate to a major disappointment than can relate to being named "Athlete of the Century."

I would never suggest that people publicly admit all their shortcomings. However, occasionally demonstrating your humanity and humility will create stronger relationships than will the sharing of all your success stories.

> People will listen a great deal more patiently
> while you explain your mistakes than
> when you explain your successes.
> —Wilbur N. Nesbit

Greasing the Skids

It is often helpful to build support for your ideas privately before seeking group approval. As an example, when I was about thirteen or fourteen, four friends and I were on our way into town.

My friend Gary Trawick pulled me off to the side and said with a grin, "Why don't we check the telephone booths and see if we can find some money?" I agreed with him, and we rejoined the others. Gary then ran his idea by the rest of the group.

I immediately said, "Yeah! That sounds like a good idea." The rest of the boys readily agreed.

By first getting me on board, my friend ran a much lower risk that someone would veto his idea or delay the decision. My immediate agreement started a feeling that his suggestion was a winner. From that experience (which netted us $3.20), I learned the value of building support for an idea before you propose it.

While serving on business or civic boards over the years, whenever I felt that a particular issue was important to the overall health of the organization, I would call a member or two before the scheduled meeting. This allowed me to build support and increase my probability of success. Also, taking this approach can bring to the surface objections you had not considered, so that you can be better prepared when they come up later in the larger group. Obtaining advance "buy-in" and support are often critical to success.

Just as there is no limit to the opportunities available, there is also no limit to the creative ideas and approaches that you can employ. Since no one tactic will work every time, you can improve your success ratio simply by increasing your options.

As a general rule the most successful man in life
is the man who has the best information.
—Benjamin Disraeli

Chapter Seven

Coaching For Success

---•---

Our chief want in life is somebody who shall
make us do what we can.
—Ralph Waldo Emerson

*Coaching other people to achieve success requires skills be-
yond simply being aware of and willing to pursue opportunities. A coach needs to understand how to create an environment
that fosters individual and collective motivation. Although it
is a challenging position, you will find few things in life more
satisfying than being able to help others develop their potential and experience success.*

*The trait of assisting others to recognize and take advan-
tage of minor, optional opportunities in preparation for those
one or two major opportunities can be as fulfilling to the coach
as to others.*

---•---

FeedbackThermostat™

The greatest opportunities for helping others to achieve success lay in providing frequent feedback. However, in most organizations, and for most people, the Feedback-Thermostat™ controls feedback. Normally, to control temperature, a thermostat is designed to come on only when it is either too hot or too cold. This same theory is often applied in the use of feedback. As a general rule, employees receive feedback only when they have exceeded a goal, gone the extra mile, or made a horrible mistake. Since most people cannot be placed in either category, they receive very limited feedback, positive or negative. However without feedback, employees tend to stop growing—they have little incentive to stretch themselves. They keep plodding along at the same rate, doing whatever they have been doing and never making any real headway.

To maximize results, your FeedbackThermostat™ should be set to motivate the masses, not to regulate the extremes. Feedback encourages people to keep improving. It is part of how they stay excited about their work. When they can see themselves growing, they tend to enjoy what they are doing more; but when they cannot see any progress, they often get discouraged and disappointed and lose much of their drive. It is an awful thing to hear someone say, "You know, I haven't learned a single new thing in years." Everyone needs to recognize their own contributions and the growth they are achieving—this is critical. If the coach points out their skills, strengths, and successes, they will reach for more opportunities, and achievement follows. With continued regular feedback, performance improves over time.

Poor Excuses

In seminars I often ask participants this question: "In your entire career, how many managers have given you effective feedback on a regular basis?" I have never seen more than two fingers raised on any participant's hands in response to this question. When I ask the reasons why managers fail to give feedback, the same answers come back again and again:

"Managers claim they are too busy—they just don't have the time."

"Managers don't know how to give feedback."

"Managers are afraid of confrontation."

"How can managers give me feedback when they don't even know what it is I do?"

Managers don't recognize the value of feedback."

"It takes effort to give effective feedback, and managers don't want to do the extra work."

"Managers feel that the organization really doesn't expect them to provide feedback, because *their* managers don't give *them* any feedback."

> **Feedback is the single greatest tool for helping others achieve success.**

These answers reveal much about the problems and opportunities attending the subject of feedback. No one can deny that effective feedback requires hard work; it is a learned skill, which must be developed and continually honed. The results, however, are worth the effort; feedback is the single greatest tool for helping others achieve success.

Upfront Expectations

The feedback process should start with the coach defining

expectations for the team member. Then, after defining the required behaviors for the job, the coach can recommend additional behaviors that the team member can consider optional, but advantageous. Studies have shown the primary reason for failure by employees is their inadequate understanding of what is expected of them. But a good coach sidesteps a host of future problems simply by never assuming that the job description and the interview process alone have adequately covered this issue.

Managers should also keep in mind that their feedback can be either required or optional. Required feedback may be the organization-mandated annual evaluation. Much more relevant and meaningful, however, is the manager's optional feedback. Because it is provided specifically to help the team members rather than to meet an organizational requirement, they value it far more.

Open to the Public

Feedback should not be limited to managers—it can come from anywhere and anyone. Once, in preparing a talk for a large technical staff supporting a sales team, I discovered that the group felt undervalued. Their managers were not on site and seldom gave them any feedback. The group felt that the salespeople were seen as the only ones who really counted in the organization, because they brought in all the money. They felt that the salespeople made unreasonable demands of them. As I went through the mental gyrations of preparing to address this group, I realized that there was one issue I could talk about that would help them: feedback. This group obviously needed feedback, but how were they going to get it? If they were not getting it from their managers, then they needed to start giving it to each other. Feedback can come from peers—it isn't just the manager's job. Often feedback has even greater value when it comes from our peers, because they may be better positioned to recognize our true contribution. We can all give feedback to one another and be the better for it, because of the opportunity for recognition and appreciation.

I have never had anyone come up to me and say, "You know, I just get too much recognition. There is always somebody coming up to me and telling me how great I am. I can't stand it anymore!" The need for positive feedback is widespread. Dr. Stephen Preas, a psychiatrist and friend of mine, once said, "In many years of practicing psychiatry, I have never had anybody come to my office suffering from stress and burnout where the root cause was overwork. In all cases, the burnout and stress were due to feeling alone and unappreciated."

While the need for positive feedback may vary among individuals, everyone needs to feel appreciated. If you want to receive more feedback, start giving more. If you want people to appreciate you, ask yourself what you are doing to show the people around you that you appreciate them. If you want people to start recognizing your strengths, prepare the ground by first pointing out the strengths of others.

Red Marks of Success

When my son was seven, he took a creative writing course. His teacher, Joyce Turrentine, was very talented, though unconventional. Instead of using a red pen to point out her students' mistakes, she circled in red the sentences she liked. Kenny would come home and exclaim, "She circled three things today!" Personally, I got a lot of red marks in school, too, but for a very different reason.

Later that same year, my son was having some problems in school. Some of his grades were not where I thought they should be. We even went so far as to ground him in order to make him improve his grades. I came home on report card day, and the first person I saw was my wife. In her hand was my son's report card, and the look on her face . . . Well, let's put it this way: no words were needed; her face said it all.

My son's report card contained the same grade that got him grounded the month before. I looked at him sternly and said, "I thought we had an understanding. I thought you were going to work harder and improve this grade."

After about thirty seconds of silence, he looked up at his mother and then at me and said, "Didn't anybody see my A's?" His words jumped out at me. I had completely overlooked his accomplishments and zeroed in on the negatives. I thought to myself, *And I teach this stuff!*

So often we point out the bad before we acknowledge the good. It starts when we are young and continues into our adult years. It seems to be our human nature to want to tell people what they did wrong, to point out their failures and identify their weaknesses. Even though 95 percent of what people do is right, we still say things like "What's wrong with this picture?" While we may find that exception reports are helpful for quickly identifying errors in systems and processes, in dealing with people there are better ways to achieve long-term improvement. Focusing on the posi- tives can make a difference.

Everyone has positive traits. The focus should start there. If you go to work each day looking for the positives, you will find them. When you really look closely at any given subject, you tend to find it everywhere. For example, before I took a job with Southern Bell, I had never noticed a Southern Bell car or truck. Soon after I joined the company, they were everywhere. When somebody tells you about a certain product, amazingly, it seems to pop up everywhere you go. When you bought your last car, how many of that model did you start to see on the highways? Were they there before, or did a million other people run out and buy the same car on the same day you did? Of course they were always there. But did you notice them before? Probably not.

By making the effort to recognize positive attributes, we encourage others as well as make them more receptive to advice.

Conventional Wisdom

One important question I often ask audiences is, "Which feedback is easier to give, negative or positive? Most will shout, "Positive!" and a few will shout, "Negative!" For those who said positive, I like to ask jokingly, "Is that why you get so much?" Conventional wisdom would suggest that positive feedback is easy to give and largely without risk. However, it isn't that simple. In today's society, we seem to have lost the ability to respond appropriately to a compliment. One reason is that many people feel awkward receiving positive feedback and believe it is best to give a humble reply. But such responses can actually serve to invalidate the person offering the compliment. For instance, Jane might say to Fred, "That was a good report you gave yesterday."

Fred may reply, "It was nothing."

Jane could interpret that as "If you think that report was good, then you really aren't that knowledgeable about reports."

Someone says, "Jim, that sure is a nice-looking shirt you have on today."

Jim retorts, "This old thing? I've had it for years." This

response puts down the complimenter, who apparently cannot even recognize when something is old or out of date.

With these typical, almost knee-jerk responses, it is easy to understand why compliments are few. Some skeptics, on receiving a compliment, are afraid to acknowledge it positively because they are not sure of the other person's motives. Many are "waiting for the other shoe to drop," expecting the positive to be followed by a negative. The good news is, there is one reply that works every time, whether the compliment was sincere or not: "Thank you!"

Several years ago, while assisting at a shelter for abused children, I noticed the following sign in the lunchroom:

> How to Accept a Compliment
> Step 1. Look at the person.
> Step 2. Smile.
> Step 3. Say, "Thank you."

I thought to myself, *This advice is not just for abused children—we all can use it.*

Don't Back Up the Truck

When you are coaching someone, keep in mind that self-improvement takes time. Don't just "back up the truck and unload." In other words, if someone has a large number of areas ripe for improvement, be careful not to point out everything wrong all at the same time. We all have egos, and most of us can only deal with a few of our weaknesses at a time. Pick out the one or two most important things, and save the others for another day. Let people experience a few successes and then a few more, until they have built a pattern of repeated successes.

The essence of genius is knowing what to overlook.
—William James

An often-taught technique is the "positive-negative-positive" approach. This approach starts feedback by pointing out one or two positive attributes, and then addresses the negatives before concluding with an additional positive. Some label this the "sandwich approach" and complain that the positives are often too superficial, causing listeners to wait for the other shoe to drop. While any approach can be taken to the extreme, the idea is first to be looking for what went right as opposed to what went wrong. Some say, "Just cut to the chase and let the person know what's wrong instead of beating around the bush." The problem with that approach is that all too often it overemphasizes the negative. Usually, if you have been around someone for a while and have been unable to identify any positives to applaud, then you have not earned the right to criticize their negatives.

Why "Good" Is Weak

Feedback gains significant power when it is specific. Feedback can be very negative or very positive, but most of the time it is neither. Frequently, it is too general to influence a person's future behavior.

Just saying "Keep up the good work" tells the listener very little. Without specific feedback, employees do not know what to keep doing, what to stop doing, or what to improve. It is much more meaningful and useful when you tell them specifically which work was good, and why. If you tell someone they did a good job, that's fine; a sincere compliment never hurts. But compare "Good job!" with this:

> "I read a letter you wrote today. I just want to let you know that I really like the way you constructed that letter. You have the ability to take complex situations and really get down to the nitty-gritty. Your style is so concise that it is truly a pleasure to read what you write."

When he gets home from work, he may shout, "Let me tell you what was said about me today!" More likely, though, he will go home and tell his wife that he had a really good day at work. That little crumb of positive feedback can literally make someone's day, and all because you were specific in your feedback. People hear it, share it, and remember it.

I once saw a cartoon of a company president walking through the office and saying to an employee, "Keep up the good work, whoever you are and whatever you do." It was a funny, but sad commentary on feedback in the workplace.

I can live for two months on a good compliment.
—Mark Twain

Bushy Eyebrows

Many times we need to check to see if what we think we have said to others is the same thing they heard and understood. Simple messages are often misinterpreted. When my daughter, Karen, was three years old, we were on our way to church, about a mile from our home. While we were sitting at a traffic light, she looked out and asked, "Do any strangers live around here?"

Looking at the house right beside us and having no idea who might live there, I answered, "Yes, some live right there."

She smiled and said, "Dad, do you know how to tell if someone is a stranger?"

Curious, I replied, "How?"

"They have very bushy eyebrows."

I had warned her about the danger of strangers; however, she was not sure what they looked like. Thus, she had developed her perception of strangers by seeing how evil cartoon characters were visually portrayed on television. Only by chance did I discover that the message I had intended regarding strangers was not the message received. It's always good to check.

Always Tell the Truth, But . . .

My grandfather had an expression that I found very insightful: "Always tell the truth, but don't always be telling it!" Some feedback you are better off not giving. It is not necessary or even helpful to provide every detail and insight when giving feedback to others. For example, after I graduated from college, I signed up to take an aptitude

> **Always tell the truth, but don't always be telling it!**

test. I was looking for a job, and no jobs were available. I really did not know what I wanted to do. The test cost $600, but for graduating seniors it was free. When I went to get my results, the adviser invited me to sit down and then asked, "Mr. Futch, did you have a difficult time in college?"

"As a matter of fact, I did," I replied, "especially in my sophomore year. However, I finished on the dean's list."

"The reason I'm asking you this question is that sometimes we give the same battery of tests to our incoming freshmen to better assess what curriculum we would suggest," he said with great concern on his face. "If we had given you this test as an incoming freshman, we would have recommended that you not attend college." I was quite taken aback.

I have often wondered why I scored that way. And it is certainly humorous now to look back on, but had I taken that aptitude test when I was an incoming freshman, it would not have been so funny. Thinking I was not "college material," I would never have gone to college. Most likely, it would have drastically changed the path I took in my life. I enjoyed college and often think about how this adviser with his negative feedback, although well intentioned, could possibly be keeping others from reaching their potential. I have often wondered just how many others may have achieved less than their potential because of feedback from an aptitude test.

Testing the Answers

If you are getting feedback from others, it is always a good idea to test it. Is this just one person's opinion, or do others feel the same way?

I remember speaking in a Toastmasters contest. I had won my chapter contest and was giving the same speech at the next level of competition. After I finished my presentation, the first person who spoke to me said, "Ken, I realize that you slowed down your presentation this time, but I still think you speak too fast. Slow down some more." The second person who spoke to me said, "Ken, you slowed it down too much this time. You need to pick that speed back up." Which person was I to believe? I considered both pieces of feedback and made my own decision, which was to return to my original speed, which I believed would work best. Using my own speed was validated by victory at the state championship.

People have varying opinions. We need to test their feedback with our known reality and with others' opinions. Our own opinions count, but remember the old adage: "If somebody calls you a horse's ass, ignore them; however, if five people call you a horse's ass, buy a saddle!"

Consider the Source

Several years ago I was invited to deliver a kickoff speech to 400 teachers in Pender County, North Carolina. I was really excited because my home town is in Pender County. My mother, who taught for forty years in the Pender school system, and my sister, who was teaching there at the time, were in attendance along with many former classmates who were either teachers or school board members.

With a built-in hometown advantage, my speech went great and was well received. I emphasized the important contributions teachers make in our society and, unfortunately, how the public fails to adequately show appreciation with rewards or recognition. I mentioned that students and former students, including me, did not always make efforts to acknowledge the impact particular teachers had on our lives. I stressed that everyone should make a habit of acknowledging the positive contributions we see others making. Then I told the audience that I wanted to follow my own advice and recognize the teacher who provided the greatest positive impact on my life. I said, "Mother, will you please stand up." At this point, all the other teachers gave my mother a standing ovation. It was truly a magical moment in my life, and one that meant the world to my mother. It is one of those rare times I will always treasure.

After my speech, we returned to my mother's home and sat talking at her kitchen table. She asked me if I had received the check for my speech. I said, "Yes, ma'am." She said, "May I see it, please?" I was a little reluctant because I had made more money in that one speech than she made teaching at that school for her entire first year. Also, some people often think speakers are overpaid, considering only the delivery time of a speech and none of the cost of doing business, which includes considerable preparation time. However, since it was my mother asking to see my check, I handed it to her. She took a long look at it and then smiled and said, "Let me say this. They got their money's worth today!" There are few things in life sweeter than to be validated by someone whom you respect and love and who also served as your greatest mentor and friend.

Feedback from those we respect is the most meaningful feedback of all. For instance, if your neighbor saw you playing basketball in your backyard and said, "You are a great basketball player," these words would not have the same impact on you as they would coming from, say, the legendary University of North Carolina Tar Heel basketball coach, Dean Smith.

You Are Above That

When my wife and I first moved into our current home, we needed some new furniture. We were fortunate to find a decorator whose recommendations always suited our tastes. Over the years, we began to depend on her advice for all our decorating needs. One day while she was visiting our home, I showed her our unfinished basement and shared with her my ideas for its completion, in hopes of gaining her advice and endorsement.

Lyse, who spoke with a beautiful French accent, gave a response that I will always remember: "No! No! No! Mr. Futch, you are above that!"

I concurred with her immediately and never again mentioned my—obviously—bad ideas, which, according to her, I was "above." Her response to my ideas, although negative, was one that appealed to my ego. She was telling me that my ideas did not match her high perception of me. I certainly did not want to pursue my original plans and have others think less of me as a result—all because Lyse had appealed to my pride.

Simple Works Best

Lowell Whitlock, the best manager/coach I ever had, did the most to improve my skills using a simple feedback process. Each month he asked me to write down and review with him what I had done the previous month as well as what I planned to do the next month. At the time, I was an instructor for AT&T, so I would write down things like "I plan to teach these classes," "I plan to develop this particular program," and "I plan to give this speech."

The first thing Lowell would do was take out the sheet of paper that I had given him the month before. He compared what I had said I was going to do with what I now said I had done.

Sometimes what I did and what I had said I was going to do were different. But that was okay. We would discuss that for a while, and then I would share what I planned to do over the next thirty days. This was not a very complex system for giving feedback, but I had never received that level of consistent feedback from a manager. So to me it was fantastic. I spent about an hour with him once a month. His simple process gave me both direction and confidence. Also, Lowell believed that every item listed as an accomplishment should be a résumé-type item. "Do it," he said, "so that when you go to interview for a job, you are ready to answer the question 'What did you accomplish in your last position?'" This also helps in documenting your yearly accomplishments when appraisal time comes along.

When Others Believe

When I was just a small child, it seemed I was always in some sort of big trouble. My greatest fear was hearing that dreaded telephone ring. I never knew when it might be someone reporting on my bad behavior.

Periodically, my mother would make her way into my bedroom just before bedtime. Because of my constant though sometimes misguided fear, her footsteps would invariably conjure up all kinds of nightmarish thoughts like, "What did I do this time?" Inside my head I would quickly run through a long list of my misdeeds for that week. Yet in spite of my numerous shortcomings and mischievous ways, rather than criticize me, my mother would always take the time to tell me how proud she was of me. She would go on and on about how pleased she was that I did not engage in many of the unbecoming activities my friends engaged in, like drinking and smoking. (I was not always entirely innocent.)

My loving mother consistently had a higher opinion of me than I deserved; she thought I was better than I actually was. She believed that I couldn't possibly have done many of the things that I in fact did do.

Did I strive to live up to her trust in me? Well, yes, I certainly sought to. Did I fall short? I must admit that many times I did. But did I retain her high esteem? Yes, that I always managed to do. And am I a better person because of her unwavering trust in me? Absolutely!

Shortly before I was to leave for Vietnam, I had a long conversation with my mother. I remember telling her that I was one of those people who really possess no special skills. She disagreed. She thought my greatest strength was my ability to get along with people. She went on to say that she had read somewhere that the primary reason most people were fired from their jobs was not incompetence, but their inability to work well with others.

At the time, I remember reflecting on her comments and realizing that indeed I had enjoyed many favors and opportunities from coworkers and managers, simply because they seemed to like me. I then concluded that this strength might not help me in Vietnam. My ability to get along would not keep the enemy from shooting me. However, I now believe it did play a role in my survival. The ability to function successfully as a team often comes down to the interpersonal skills of the members, particularly the leaders. While I could not convince the enemy not to shoot, I was fortunate enough to lead a team that protected each member. My mother, in helping me to realize my strengths, inspired me to use my skills to build a healthy team environment.

The first step to believing in ourselves often comes from

having others believe in us. We have the power to express our faith in others, which affects how they see themselves. And we all need to find others who believe in us, too. Supportive friends and mentors are essential to success in life and work.

People become really quite remarkable when
they start thinking that they can do things.
When they believe in themselves,
they have the first secret of success.
—Norman Vincent Peale

In 1969, Robert Rosenthal, a professor of social psychology at Harvard University, began an experiment to test the "Pygmalion Effect" (self-fulfilling prophecy) in the classroom. Rosenthal told each teacher in a selected elementary school that a special test had revealed that 20 percent of her students were "intellectual bloomers." He assured these teachers that the identified pupils, entirely on their own, would show remarkable gains in intelligence in the next eight months. Actually, the children had been chosen at random. The only real difference between them and their classmates was the perception planted in the minds of their teachers. At the end of the school term, a test revealed that those labeled "bloomers" really had bloomed by gaining, on average, four more IQ points compared to their classmates. The experimental Pygmalion results were impressive and proved that we can all influence the success of other people simply by our belief in them. These students excelled because they were expected to excel and because at least one person believed they would succeed.

Through an unexpected situation, I found the transforming power of having others believe in me. In Officer Candidate School, one of my weaknesses was my inability to read maps. When I got to Vietnam, I went on my first outing by myself and promptly got lost. I realized I was lost when told to check a particular location believed to be the source of enemy radio signals. I went to the suspected location and radioed back that there was nothing there. When I tried to return to my original location, I decided to go back a different way, by following a river. Only when I came to a fork in the river did I realize that where I thought I was and where I actually was were two different places. In fact, the "enemy" radio signals being received at the base camp were actually coming from my radio. This experience did nothing to boost my self-confidence in my map-reading abilities.

Two days later I was back with my company commander. We were traveling in company formation, with my platoon in the lead. I was terrified. Now I feared the whole world would find out that I did not know how to read a map! I was going to be leading the entire company and had no idea how to take us where we needed to go. We traveled all morning without incident. Around noon, we approached a large river. We decided to break for lunch, and I went back to discuss with the captain the best way to cross the river. While we reviewed this, I happened to overhear the first sergeant talking with a group of enlisted men. "I'm damn glad we finally got a lieutenant in here" (me) "who knows what the hell he's doing. This one's got a little age on him." (I was the grand old age of twenty-three.) "It's about time they sent us someone who knows how to read a map."

I thought, "Well, this sergeant has been in the army for twenty years, and if he thinks I can read a map, then obviously I'm mistaken to think I can't read a map." From that point on, I never made another error in map reading. Frequently, we need other people to believe in us first, before we are able to believe in ourselves. Their belief in us is critical to our self-confidence. Taking your best shot starts with believing you are capable of shooting.

> The first and most important step toward success
> is the feeling that we can succeed.
> —Nelson Boswell

Money, Money, Money

The motivating difference between someone who performs well and someone who performs poorly is not how much they are paid, but how they are treated. I often like to ask audiences what motivates them. The replies usually include "money." Some say, "Keep your trash, trinkets, and T-shirts. Just give me the cash."

I like to point out how it is possible to give someone a ten-thousand-dollar raise and at the same time depress them rather than motivate them. Let me elaborate. Imagine that you work for me, and I call you into my office and say, "Susie, you did a great job this year, and to show you that it's not just talk, I am going to back my words up with a ten-thousand-dollar raise." I then point to an audience member and ask, "How would that make you feel?"

Invariably the audience member says, "Great!"

Continuing my example, I tell them how Susie walks down the hall to Bob's office and says, "Guess what? I just got a ten-thousand-dollar raise."

"Just ten? The rest of us got twenty."

Guess who has become disappointed and depressed and is thinking about quitting her job. What happened to the motivation that should have resulted from a hefty raise?

I do believe that money is often a stimulator, but only over the short term. Money can be compared to air-conditioning. For example, let us say you are working in a building without air-conditioning, and someone from headquarters comes out for a visit with the intent of helping to improve morale. They may ask what could be done to make the job better. Your response might be, "Air-conditioning would be great . . . We're about to burn up!"

You would be absolutely correct in your thinking—air-conditioning would improve morale for that location. Then I like to ask, "Since most of you currently work in air-conditioned offices, when is the last time you saw someone run through the office proclaiming, 'I love working here because it's so nice and cool!'" If they did, I'm sure someone would quickly take them away to the psych ward. Once something is taken for granted, it fails to motivate, but take that something away, and it never fails to discourage.

So it is with money. Even if you get a raise, you quickly get accustomed to your increased salary and your lifestyle changes. Pretty soon you no longer realize or appreciate the pay increase. Any motivation you felt on receiving the raise is long forgotten.

Money plays a role in motivation, but not always for the obvious reasons. Money is often the way we keep score—by measuring and comparing individuals' contributions. As a result, we like money because we see it as a way to be recognized and rewarded for our value and contributions. This recognition is usually more important than the tangible value of the money.

Money was never a big motivation for me,
except as a way to keep score.
The real excitement is playing the game.
—Donald Trump

I served on the salary review committee for a church during a period of declining donations. At the end of the year, we decided that we could not really afford to spend the amount of money needed for the annual raises that the staff deserved. We agreed on a small, three percent across-the-board salary increase for everyone. One member disagreed, saying that he thought raises based on merit would be a better approach. However, he went along with the plan for the across-the-board raises.

The next year, donations declined even further, so we decided that we could not give any raises at all, except to two individuals whose salaries were ridiculously low. The committee member who had recommended the merit raise idea the previous year missed the meeting when this decision was made. During the following meeting, after our decisions had been announced, he erroneously commented in front of everyone that he was glad we had chosen merit raises this year. The church secretary, on hearing his comment, quit the next day. She thought her efforts were not adequately recognized or appreciated. It was not about money for her; it was about recognition and appreciation. She believed her contributions were not valued or appreciated.

Happy for a Life Time

I once heard a psychologist say, "If you want to be happy for an hour, take a nap. If you want to be happy for a day, go fishing. If you want to be happy for a week, take a vacation. If you want to be happy for a month, get married. If you want to be happy for a lifetime, learn to love what you do."

We have always been told that money may not buy happiness, but when have we heard that happiness can buy money? There is a strong correlation between enjoyment and success. Albert Schweitzer said, "Success is not the key to happiness. Happiness is the key to success. If you love what you are doing, you will be successful."

The importance of enjoying a job should never be underestimated. Too many people fail to derive any enrichment from their chosen careers. Once, **Money may not buy happiness, but happiness can buy money.**
a man in one of my classes told me, "I hated this job the first day I came, and I have hated all thirty years I've been here. All I want is to retire and get my pension."

I remember thinking, "You poor fool! There's no guarantee you will even live to retirement." Life is way too short to spend the majority of your time being miserable. When you consider how much of your life is spent on the job, it is dreadfully foolish to only seek enjoyment away from work. While it is unreasonable to expect to enjoy every aspect of work, a significant portion of it should be rewarding.

I believe that to enjoy a job requires interesting work, a sense of accomplishment, and a feeling of being appreciated. Determining what constitutes interesting work is very subjective and personal—what one person finds interesting may be a frightful bore to someone else. There is far greater commonality, however, in people's need for the other two requisites: a sense of accomplishment and a feeling of appreciation.

Taking your best shot sometimes requires using someone else's ammunition.

Individuals will always bear the ultimate responsibility for their own achievement and enjoyment. A coach, however, can play a strong supporting role by helping individuals to achieve success and feel appreciated.

A coach, by developing the habit of giving frequent feedback, can create a stimulating environment. Feedback is contagious and can rapidly spread throughout an organization. Effective feedback not only accelerates the learning process, but also helps individuals to feel appreciated for their contributions.

As we learn to recognize opportunities, whether minor or major, we also can help others recognize their opportunities. By refining our feedback skills, we are able to help others not only to achieve personal growth, but also to visualize how their talents might be a fit for a potential opportunity. Taking your best shot sometimes requires using someone else's ammunition; a coach can often provide the bullets.

There is no such thing as a "self-made" man.
We are made up of thousands of others. Everyone
who has ever done a kind deed for us, or spoken
one word of encouragement to us, has entered
into the make-up of our character and of
our thoughts, as well as our success.
—George Matthew Adams

Chapter Eight

Expectations for Leaders

Leaders help others to succeed.
—Erin Templet

In a leadership role, greater expectations come with the position. And because situational opportunities are constantly changing, the leader's behaviors must also change to meet them. The following situations illustrate how both required and optional behaviors can influence your success as a leader.

Giving Your Rifle Away

One hot, muggy day while I was leading our weary platoon through the jungles, we were caught in an ambush by a large force of North Vietnamese Army regulars. Luckily, the opening onslaught of rifle fire went over our heads, allowing us to take cover and return fire. The enemy seemed to have a tendency to shoot too high. We never knew why, but our theory was that it had something to do with our height, since we were generally much taller than they. Shooting high must have seemed logical to them.

In this ambush, we were able to survive by returning a blistering level of firepower including rifle, mortar, and artillery. Eventually, we forced the enemy to retreat. During this horrendous firefight, there were two high-stress incidents I will take with me to my grave. The first incident occurred while flanking a squad around to the right. One of my sergeants faced a situation that many of us feared—while crawling he found himself eyeball to eyeball with a bamboo viper.

We had been told upon arrival in Vietnam that there were two kinds of snakes: three-steppers and five-steppers. It had been explained to us that when bitten by a three-stepper, you would only take three steps before falling over dead. Now, with the five-stepper you got those all-important two additional steps. What did this young sergeant do when he encountered the snake? He let out a bloodcurdling scream that shook the foundations of hell, then he jumped straight up! He explained later that he was more afraid of the snake than of the bullets. His scream, however, led me to believe he had been shot and was in need of assistance and possible medical evacuation.

Right after receiving word he was uninjured, the second major event brought home an important lesson. A man began yelling that his M16 rifle had jammed. At that particular moment, I was on the radio directing artillery and requesting more ammunition from the rear. I tossed him my rifle, and he continued to return fire. Later that evening, after repairing his rifle, he returned my rifle with a smile and said, "Thanks." I decided that since I didn't need a rifle in one of our toughest fights, perhaps I didn't need one at all. For the balance of my tour in Vietnam, I carried only a .45-caliber pistol.

My responsibility as combat leader was not to fire my rifle

at the enemy. My job was to direct the platoon's activities, to keep our line even (to help prevent friendly-fire accidental shootings that could result from someone being too far up or too far back), and to be in communication with artillery, mortar, and air support. If I was engaged in shooting my rifle, there were more important activities that I was neglecting.

Job clarity, understanding of roles, and a willingness to perform primary functions are always a leader's primary responsibilities. In corporate America, leaders often perform tasks that should be done by others. I often saw sales managers, when accompanying a salesperson, take over the role of the salesperson. While some situations may require this drastic step, it usually can be avoided. Managers too frequently look for a reason to do what they do best. People naturally gravitate into their comfort zone. Sales managers often get their jobs because they are the best salespeople in the organization. For new sales managers, transforming sales skills into management skills is a real challenge. The continuing desire of a sales manager to demonstrate his or her sales ability often works to the detriment of the salespeople as well as the manager. Too often the best salespeople do not make the best sales managers because transition into leadership does not occur.

> **Sometimes, taking your best shot means being willing to give up your gun.**

When you receive your promotion, demonstrate your trust and hand over your rifle. Give it to the person who needs it most. Make sure you stay focused on your mission of directing your team, and keep the ammunition coming. Sometimes, taking your best shot means being willing to give up your gun.

Good-Luck Piece

When I was about ten, my father built a camp right next to the Northeast Cape Fear River. It was just seven miles from our house, and on occasion my dad would allow my friends and me to spend the night there alone. We would get up bright and early the next morning to go fishing.

Once when I was just thirteen years old, my father took a couple of my friends and me up to the camp for an overnight trip. I remembered the small country store that was just a short distance away, and knew we would want to buy some drinks and honey buns the next morning. My father was about to leave when I asked, "Daddy, do you think I could have some money? The country store has great honey buns, you know . . ."

My dad looked down at me and smiled as he reached into his pocket. His hand came out empty. "Son, I'm sorry," he said, "I don't have a penny on me."

I must have looked pretty sad because I saw my dad looking at me in sympathy. "Wait a minute," he said, reaching into his back pocket and pulling out his wallet. He flipped open one of its secret compartments and pulled out an old fifty-cent piece. With a big smile on his face, he said, "Here, take this."

"Daddy," I replied, "isn't that the fifty-cent piece that has your birth date on it? The one Granny gave you when you were a just a kid—the one you've kept for all these years?"

"Yeah, but that's okay."

"No way. Daddy, I won't take your good-luck piece; I'll just borrow some money from the other guys."

My father looked down at me, gave an approving smile, and said, "Okay, son."

I learned a valuable lesson that day—one of love, sacrifice, and putting others' needs first. This act of selflessness and willingness to sacrifice demonstrated my father's value system as he played the part of role model, guiding and shaping my growth as a person.

Walking Point

While moving through the jungle, the "point man"—so named because he went in first—had, without a doubt, the most dangerous job in the platoon. He would be the first to spring a booby trap, step on a land mine, or surprise enemy soldiers heading down the trail toward us. A long-standing tradition in our company was that newcomers would quickly be trained to perform this difficult task. This was done so that soldiers nearing the end of their tour could be spared this high-risk activity. The idea was simple: it was better to die in your first month in Vietnam than in your last month. Nothing seemed worse than the possibility of spending eleven months in hell and then getting killed.

Our traveling protocol was for the platoon leader (lieutenant) to walk behind the last man in the first squad. In my platoon we had three squads of approximately thirteen men. The platoon sergeant also walked behind the last squad so he was available in case of a casualty to the platoon leader.

Frequently, the point man would need further instructions in order to deal with obstacles on the trail, possible booby traps, or the trail splitting into multiple directions. As the platoon leader, when such situations arose, the point man would call me on the radio for advice, which sometimes required a "look-see." After walking up to the front and determining the action needed, our platoon would start moving again. I would then wait until the last man in the first squad passed me before taking my place in the line. On days I was called to the front multiple times for decisions, I sometimes would not wait for the last man to pass before I got in line. This seemed to save time if I felt that another decision requiring a "look-see" was imminent. Also, when it was getting late in the day and navigational decisions were difficult, I would simply stay at the front and sometimes even walk point myself. I did this because with me personally walking point, it seemed to expedite our arrival times—it was a lot easier to set up positions for the evening when there was still daylight left.

One evening during a conversation, my captain said, "Rumor has it that you sometimes walk point."

"Only a few times," I confessed.

"In case you've forgotten, the Army has a significant training investment in you. While I know you're aware of the already high-risk nature of your job, you should not make it worse. Walking point isn't your job!" He went on to add, "You do *not* have the right to unnecessarily put Army resources at risk. Do you understand the Army's position and why you should not walk point in the future?"

"I hadn't thought about it like that," I admitted. "It won't happen again."

As I look back, I realize I was fortunate that neither the Army nor I suffered as a result of my taking avoidable risks. However, I also understand I derived a huge benefit from voluntarily walking point. That benefit was the respect I earned from my men. My men knew I was not asking them to do anything that I was not willing to do myself.

It is not fair to ask of others what
you are not willing to do yourself.
—Eleanor Roosevelt

In working with others, no matter what role we play, it is important that the others on our team not feel that we consider ourselves above doing difficult or menial tasks. Some of the greatest leaders I have ever had the pleasure to work with were ones who arrived early, made coffee, and poured it for everyone else. This optional behavior conveyed a mind-set of service. Leadership will always be about serving, not about being served.

Making Others Guess

An executive of a large company engaged my consulting services to improve the quality of his staff's technical sales presentations. The staff was routinely asked to prepare presentations for him to deliver to the Pentagon. These presentations involved large government contracts. He believed his staff was oblivious to what was needed in a professional sales presentation. He complained of not receiving visual aids with concise points. Instead he got "data dumps." The staff's poor efforts forced him to spend a major amount of his personal time simplifying their materials into effective and deliverable presentations. He asked me to design a training program that would solve his problem. I agreed and received his permission to meet individually with his staff members before developing a class.

In asking his staff members how they currently prepared presentations for their boss, I discovered the real problem. I became acutely aware of the difficulty of their challenge. When told to prepare a presentation on a particular topic such as fiber-optic switching, staff members were never informed why the presentation was needed or how it would be used. Therefore, they simply regurgitated everything they knew on the subject and hoped it would be sufficient. They had no understanding of what was required of them, and thus provided inadequate presentation material.

I met with the executive again and asked about the directions he gave his staff. Then I explained their current understanding.

He said, "I shouldn't have to tell them every single point about how to prepare a presentation. They should already know this!"

"Have you ever showed your staff your changes after revamping their presentations?"

"No."

"So they never see the final product."

"I'm too busy to spend time on such trivial matters."

Having already talked with his people, I realized they were all bright and capable, but extremely intimidated. I knew that training was not the answer to this problem. I recommended simply describing his expectation and then showing his staff the improvements he made, so they would understand what he needed. That way, they would be equipped to meet his expectations.

The team members did not understand what their leader needed, wanted, or expected from them. They knew he was unhappy with them, but did not really know why. Your team members cannot effectively recognize a potential opportunity unless they first understand your expectations.

What Side Is Your Heart On

Ralph Thompson, a man in his late sixties, worked at my father's service station for a number of years. Ralph was responsible for teaching me the importance of concern for others. On occasion he would ask me to buy him a Pepsi, and sometimes I would. Other times I would say I could not, because I was "broke." What made his request interesting is that sometimes when I responded, "Sure," he would quickly answer, "That's okay; I just wanted to see what side your heart was on." He made these small requests often enough that I never knew the true motivation behind each request.

Ralph provided me with many opportunities to demonstrate my concern for his welfare. He taught me that a willingness to share was sometimes as important as actually sharing. Ralph knew that the sum of the minor situations told the real story: did I have his best interest at heart?

No one will care how much you know,
until they know how much you care.
—Gerhard Gschwandtner

The Value of Foxholes

In some situations, success depends on your ability to see the value in the boring and unpleasant activities. In the jungles of Vietnam, at the end of every day while on search-and-destroy missions, we had to prepare our defense for the coming night. Like western settlers circling their covered wagons, we would form a circle and dig in for the night.

The ground was often very hard, making the digging of foxholes a long and arduous task. Foxholes had to be big enough and numerous enough to accommodate everyone. They served two purposes. First, they had to be strategically located so that rifle fire from the foxhole could protect our perimeter from ground attacks. Also, they had to provide protection for everyone in case of incoming mortar attacks. To accomplish this, the foxholes had to be deep enough so that you could get your entire body below the surface of the ground. Usually, two to four soldiers would share the digging of the foxhole—and its safety in the event of an attack.

There was never a problem getting the men to dig foxholes the evening following a night attack.

I could tell how long a soldier had been in Vietnam by looking at the foxholes he dug. When he first arrived, he would dig it the way he had been taught. However, after a period of time without being attacked at night—and thus not needing to use the foxholes that had been so laboriously dug—many soldiers began to think the digging was a waste of time and effort. So their foxholes got to be smaller and smaller. Sometimes, while inspecting the perimeter security, I would come upon a foxhole that was about three feet long and fifteen inches deep.

"Whose foxhole is this?"

Four people replied, "It's ours."

"And you think it's big enough?"

"Oh, yes, sir!"

"Okay, get in it, and let's see." It is a funny sight to see four grown men try to fit into a ridiculously small hole!

As I laughed, they shot back, "Well, if live rounds were coming in, we could get a lot lower."

"Yeah, right. Now, dig it deeper and longer."

Occasionally, I would come to a foxhole that was about six feet deep, with logs pulled over the top of it. That foxhole would belong to a couple of guys who had been in Vietnam for eleven months and did not want to take any chance of getting killed the last few weeks they were there. I would say, "You can't shoot out of this hole at anything that's not standing right on top of you. Now, fill it in some, so you can stand up and see out of it, in case we get a ground attack."

People will not always automatically do what is best for themselves or their organization, particularly if the work is difficult or the necessity of it is in question. There was never a problem getting the men to dig foxholes the evening following a night attack. It was only a problem when it had been days since a night attack, and my soldiers' perception of the need for the foxholes had changed. My expectations concerning the depth and length of the foxholes never varied. I was committed to getting my men— and me—out of Vietnam alive. I knew our odds of survival were increased by my insisting on adequate foxholes every night.

There are certain situations where success depends on doing the basics even when the basics are not always valued. Although my continued focus on the foxholes was not always appreciated, it achieved its purpose night after night. We all got out alive.

Leaders, like all team members, must meet certain expectations. The basics, while not always easy, must be done. Understanding the importance of fulfilling both required and optional behaviors increases your opportunity for success.

Leadership is getting someone to do
what they don't want to do,
to achieve what they want to achieve.
—former Dallas Cowboys coach Tom Landry

Chapter Nine

Negative Situations

———————————•———————————

Any fact facing us is not as important as our attitude toward it,
for that determines our success or failure.
—Norman Vincent Peale

Seeing the opportunity in negative situations is not only dif-
ficult; it is not something that most of us intuitively grasp. In
most cases it is a learned behavior. Seeing the opportunity imme-
diately, at the time the negative is occurring, is even more diffi-
cult. Opportunity recognition again plays a pivotal role in
achieving success.

It Was Just Right

During my tenure at Futch's ESSO, Ralph, the service station worker, taught me how to analyze situations and see
benefits in both the good and the bad. Just before we closed the
station one Saturday evening in July, a local lawyer stopped by
for gas on his way home. The lawyer gave Ralph the better portion of a fifth of bourbon. The following week that same lawyer

———————————•———————————

stopped by for more gas, and on seeing Ralph, he asked, "How was the liquor I gave you?"

Ralph responded, "Well, Mr. Corbett, it was just right."

"What do you mean by 'just right'?" inquired Mr. Corbett.

"Well, if it had been any better, you wouldn't have given it to me, and if it had been any worse, I couldn't have drunk it. It was just right!"

In every situation there are both positives and negatives. No single person or situation is perfect. There are lessons to be learned from each situation and from every person you come in contact with—the key is to be looking for the lessons.

We all find ourselves in unexpected situations that we would not have chosen. Some are painful, with very negative consequences. The downside of these events is usually quite obvious, for we readily recognize the negatives. The opportunities, though, are often hidden or delayed and sometimes only become clear in retrospect. With the passage of time, we are able to place the event in a larger picture, like fitting a puzzle piece. The more quickly we can recognize and assess even minor negative opportunities, the sooner we position ourselves for more success.

These days when I have a really bad customer-service experience, I almost enjoy it—I can nearly always find great material from it to include in a speech. For example, I went to meet a client for lunch at one of Atlanta's upscale hotels. The client was delayed, and I decided to use the time to get a shoeshine. When I climbed up into the chair, this nice-looking young woman glanced up at me and asked, "Did anyone ever tell you that you look like Bill Murray?"

"Yes, a few people have mentioned it."

To my surprise she replied, "He sure is ugly." She must have realized her faux pas and followed up with, "I'm not saying you're ugly, just that he is."

I thought, *Then what are you saying? This is not a great way to get tips.*

As I sat in my chair pondering, I began to smile. *This is good! I can use this.*

While we can't always find the humor in every negative situation, there may still be an opportunity—if we can get a new perspective. There are so many situations that we cannot change; bad things do happen. But we always have a choice: to bemoan our misfortunes or to see them as the breeding ground for new opportunities. Hopefully, we will not have to deal with too many of the really major negatives, but we can count on an abundance of minor inconvenient,

> **Bad things do happen. But we always have a choice: to bemoan our misfortunes or to see them as the breeding ground for new opportunities.**

embarrassing, or annoying situations. These everyday "minor negatives" should be our training ground for the much rarer, but more daunting, major situations. This doesn't mean that just looking for the opportunities will allow you to sail merrily through life's heaviest seas, but you will be in a better position to reap the unexpected rewards.

When You Say Whiskey

Because life is always full of surprises, flexibility helps enormously. The ability to quickly see both sides of an issue or a situation can be very rewarding.

The following story is my all-time favorite about someone demonstrating flexibility.

A small-town newspaper editor had the audacity to ask the town's favorite politician, during a political campaign, where he stood on the "issue of whiskey." Giving an answer to this question always put one in the situation of "damned if you do and damned if you don't," but I'll never forget how this great North Carolina politician handled the question. He demonstrated the very essence of flexibility. His response went something like this:

"Sir, I had not planned to discuss such a controversial issue at this time, but far be it from me to sidestep any issue, regardless of the nature and regardless of the consequence. First, I want to make sure that I understand you, sir. If, sir, when you say whiskey, you mean that devil's brew, that poisonous scourge, that bloody monster that defiles innocents, that destroys reason, creates misery and poverty, and takes the very bread out of the mouths of babes.

"Sir, if, when you say whiskey, you mean that vile drink that topples the Christian man and woman from the very pinnacle of righteous and gracious living into the bottomless pit of despair, shame, degradation, hopelessness, and helplessness; destroys homes, creates orphans, and depraves the community in general . . .

"Sir, if that's what you mean by whiskey, I want you to put in your paper that I promise my con-

- continued -

stituents, if I'm elected, I'll fight to destroy this demon with all the strength that I possess!

"However, on the other hand, if, when you say whiskey, you mean that oil of conversation, that philosophic wine and ale which is consumed when good friends get together, that drink that puts a song in their hearts and laughter on their lips; if you mean that blessed substance that enables a poor man to embrace a few of the simple pleasures of this earth and to forget, if only for a moment, the heartaches, trials, and tribulations of this world.

"Sir, if you mean the medicinal spirit that puts a spring in the old man's step on a frosty morn, if you mean that nectar of the gods, the sale of which puts untold millions in our treasuries, provides tender care for the little orphan children, the blind, and the deaf, the aged, and the infirmed, builds highways, hospitals, and schools, and makes this world a better place in which to live . . .

"Sir, If that's what you mean by whiskey, I want you to put in your paper that I promise my constituents, if I'm elected, I'll FIGHT to protect this essence of divinity with all the strength that I possess."

Then he added a crowning finale: "Now that I have answered your query without equivocation, I feel you should, in all good conscience, put in your

- continued -

> newspaper that I'm a man with the courage of my convictions. This is my stand; I will not compromise."
>
> He won every election he ever ran in!

This master orator was eloquent and passionate about both sides of the issue. Obviously, there will always be more than one way to look at any situation.

Monkey Habits

In situations where we find ourselves struggling to deal with a major change in our lives, we may need to analyze our emotional attachments to the past. Often, by clinging to the past we can miss the opportunities surrounding us right now.

Before going to Vietnam, I was sent to jungle survival school in Panama. The site was selected because its jungles were considered more difficult to navigate than the ones we would experience in Vietnam. The training included how to survive without food rations in the jungle. We were told to remember a five-step process for determining which foods were edible.

Step 1. Visual: Does it look appetizing?

Step 2. Smell: Does it smell pungent or sweet?

Step 3. Taste: Touching your tongue to it, does it taste bitter or sweet?

Step 4. Mini-trial: Take a very small bite, chew, swallow, and wait for twenty minutes. Do you feel sick?

Step 5. Consume: Eat a larger portion and feel fairly confident that what you have eaten is not poisonous.

We were told that a better way to determine whether a food was poisonous was to feed some to someone else and see what happened to them.

We were also warned against going by what animals consumed. Our Panamanian instructor, in his broken English, said, "You see monkeys pick 'em berries and put in mouth. You say, 'Aha, me eat berries.' You eat berries—you die. You say, 'Why, monkey no die?' Because monkey no eat berries. Monkey put berries in mouth and play with dem like marbles. When you no look, monkey spit dem out. No eat what monkey eat; eat monkey."

He went on to say, "Now let me teach you how to catch monkey. Take coconut and make hole in shell jus' big enough for monkey's hand. Den, place shiny t'ing in coconut shell. It can be C-ration top, aluminum foil, anyt'ing shiny. Den, tie coconut shell to stake in ground. Monkey come by and spy shiny t'ing. Monkey must have shiny t'ing. So, monkey stick hand in coconut shell and grab shiny t'ing. When monkey make fist, he no can get hand out of coconut. Monkey pull. Monkey jerk. Monkey jump, but monkey no turn 'em loose. Monkey must have shiny t'ing. You come next morning. Monkey see you come, and he get mad. Monkey scream. Monkey pick up rock and t'row at you. Monkey pick up stick and t'row at you. You pick up bigga stick. Knock monkey in head. Eat monkey."

I was relieved that I never had to resort to looking for edible berries or trapping monkeys for my survival. However, it has been my experience that many people are like the monkeys—they hold on to something for too long. This is particularly true when it comes to how people respond to change. Many people hate change, even when the change is in their own best interest. By releasing its hold and pulling its hand out of the coconut shell, the monkey could have gotten free. Instead, because of its stubborn desire to have the "shiny thing," it stayed trapped. Sometimes people need to let go of something in the past to which they have an emotional attachment. That's *their* "shiny thing." I have seen people become attached to buildings, desks, a particular cubicle space, a way of doing things, an old boss—the list goes on. Opportunity analysis often requires us to determine what past connections are keeping us from embracing new opportunities.

> The problem is never how to get new, innovative thoughts
> into your mind, but how to get old ones out.
> —Dee Hock, Founder of Visa

Ida, I Hear Something

As my grandfather aged, he developed cataracts on both eyes, destroying nearly all of his vision. My grandmother's sight remained fairly strong all her life, but her hearing deteriorated. One afternoon when I was a teenager, I decided to drive over for a short visit with them. As I pulled my car into their driveway and opened the door, I could hear their TV blasting *The Price is Right* to the world. I walked up their back steps and found the back door locked. As I looked in, I could see them both seated in their favorite chairs, watching television with the volume at full blast. I began pounding on the door. Finally, after the third flurry of loud banging, I saw my grandfather flinch and begin to look around, motioning to my grandmother. He then yelled, "Ida! Ida!

I hear something! Do you see anything?"

I have always thought that was a prime example of teamwork. It also went well beyond teamwork to demonstrate how, in facing negative situations, we must always be receptive to new approaches in order to solve new challenges.

My grandparents' physical abilities changed over time, creating the need for a complementary alliance. Between the two of them, they had good vision and good hearing, both of which were needed for them to get along in their later years. Neither was complete alone. For others of us, dealing with change may mean acquiring new skills that were not needed before, or forming new partnerships or alliances in order to take advantage of a new situation.

Mother's Funeral

Life often surprises us with both good and bad situations. Our challenge is to remain vigilant for the opportunities in all situations. Occasionally, opportunities will accompany even the worst circumstances.

Around two a.m. on Monday, March 4, 2002, I got a telephone call informing me that Mother had just passed away. The news was cushioned by the knowledge that my mother had been in terrible pain for the past several months, and there was no hope for improvement. Still, losing one's mother is never easy.

Several weeks earlier, knowing that the end was near, my sisters had asked if I wanted to deliver a eulogy at her funeral. As I drove to North Carolina that morning to join my family members, I began to think about what I would say. Though I knew that delivering this eulogy would be a difficult challenge, I also knew there was no way I could refuse the opportunity to honor my mother. I felt an overwhelming obligation to do what I do best—speak—and to pay tribute to her in the best way I could.

When the funeral service started and we began to sing my mother's favorite hymns, I became so emotional that I struggled to hold the hymnal steady and was too choked up to sing. I then began to wonder if my decision to speak was in fact a good idea. After the two Methodist ministers finished their sermons, I left my family and walked up to the pulpit. The church, along with the overflow rooms, was filled to capacity, with the majority of attendees being her former students. As I stood there looking at all those faces, I was reminded again of our collective purpose that day, to show our respect for an extraordinary woman. I knew then that nothing could prevent me from delivering my words in her memory and honor. Not until later would I understand that having the courage to stand and deliver the following eulogy would be one of the greatest opportunities of my life.

Excerpt from the Elizabeth C. Futch Eulogy

While nearly everyone thinks their mother is great, I believe Mother was truly an extraordinary individual. I have decided to list the attributes that I believe best describe her, and then use examples and stories to illustrate and validate my selections.

Intellect: Mother attended eleven different schools as a result of her father's job. Yet she still managed to graduate with honors at age fifteen from a twelve-grade school system. At nineteen

- continued -

she became a high school teacher after graduating from college with a triple major (math, English, and history). She was only one course short of another major, in Latin, and obtained the highest academic average in the history of her college.

Prepared: Mother believed in doing your homework. This morning I went alone to the funeral home to say my final good-bye. As I stood by her coffin, telling her again how grateful I was to have had such a wonderful mother and how much I loved her, I told her that I was going to do my best to honor her today. At that moment, I could hear her saying what she had always said to me before I attempted any challenge: "Are you prepared?" Knowing that I still had not finalized my comments, I smiled and said, "Not yet." At this point, I heard her give me her final advice: "Well, why are you standing here? Go home and get prepared!"

Teacher: She was a schoolteacher for forty-six years. Not only did she possess an extraordinary grasp of mathematical concepts, she was greatly skilled in conveying that knowledge to others. Teaching six math classes a day, assigning daily homework in all of them, and then grading every student's work exemplified her dedication to her job and to her students. Over her career she received hundreds of letters from former students, crediting her for their later success in both college and careers.

- continued -

She also taught her own children in school. I had my mother for Algebra I, Algebra II, Plane Geometry, Solid Geometry, and Trigonometry. Unlike my sisters, my presence seemed to provide Mother a greater challenge. For example, a student in my class asked Mother how to work a particularly difficult homework problem. After using the entire blackboard to complete the appropriate equation, Mother realized she had made an error. So she paused and stepped back to review her work. In the ensuing silence a sarcastic voice said, "How do you expect us to work it, if you can't?"

Mother spun around, frowned, and firmly stated, "Wayne Cowan, let me tell you something!"

Wayne immediately pointed directly at me, exclaiming, "It wasn't me! It was him!"

She then looked at me and said, "Young man, I will tend to you when I get you home!" And she did!

Contributor: After her retirement, Mother continued to find ways to contribute to the community. At eighty-six, she still served on the Board of Adult Services, delivered meals on wheels, taught Sunday school, sang in the choir, and taught adult literacy. All the while she visited everyone she knew who was sick or homebound. I once asked, upon seeing her particularly tired, "Mother, I thought you were retired." She quickly responded, "I just can't see Jesus retiring, or saying, 'Well, I have done

- continued -

enough good; I think I'll just kick back and play some golf.' As long as you are alive and able, you should be making a contribution."

Generous: As a retired schoolteacher, Mother had little money. However, with few bills and a conservative lifestyle, she found herself having more disposable income in retirement than in any other period of her life. She said that what she enjoyed most about having extra money was being able to give more to charity. Looking at her checkbook, we learned that in addition to her tithe to the church, she had contributed to over fifty different charities in her last year of life.

Well-traveled: With a daughter working for the State Department and living in many foreign countries, my mother took every opportunity to visit her, plus take additional side trips. At seventy-five, she and her college roommate, both widowed for many years, went with a tour group to Europe. While in Paris, they visited a famous nightclub. I later asked mother if she enjoyed the nightclub. "Oh, yes," she responded, "the music and dancing were absolutely fabulous. However, I could have done without the nudity!"

Positive: She was never one to complain; although she experienced her share of pain. When Mother was ten years of age, her mother died; at thirteen, her brother died; at nineteen, her father died, and at fifty-two, her husband died. Although

- continued -

involved in some serious accidents, along with a painful disease that ended her life, she would never mention being in pain unless someone inquired. Even then her comments were brief.

Consistent: Mother's actions corresponded with her intentions. Words never heard from Mother: "I really need to take a dish to that family, but I am just too tired." If mother thought she needed to do something, she did it.

Most people *know* the right thing.
Many people *try* to do the right thing.
Mother *did* the right thing.

If you ever wonder what a difference one person can make, remember Betty Futch.

It has been said that when you are born, you are crying while others are smiling, and that you should live your life so that when you die, you are smiling while others are crying.

Today we know you are smiling.

Upon leaving the church, an eighty-five-year-old woman approached me saying, "Young Kenny, I've been to many a funeral in my life, but this is the first one that I ever enjoyed."

My mother's death provided me a major opportunity to help show honor and respect to the person who had given me life and who continuously enriched my life. All the speeches and seminars that I delivered and had perceived as major opportunities at the time morphed into minor opportunities. They were the preparation for my greatest opportunity. She had lived an extraordinary life that deserved to be acknowledged and celebrated, and I feel blessed to have been able to recognize and respond to that great opportunity.

Many concepts sound easy until we find ourselves face-to-face with an emotional situation. Looking for opportunities in negative situations requires making a conscious effort, because seeing the positives with the negatives is seldom a natural response. However, focusing on the obstacles usually delays and can even obliterate potential opportunity. Alexander Graham Bell once said, "When one door closes, another door opens; but we often look so long and so regretfully upon the closed door that we do not see the ones which open for us."

Far more important than what has happened to us in life is how we respond to it.

Our view of the past deeply affects how we see the future. For some, it can be the "glory days" that overshadow and minimize the present. Trying to recapture this past period is invariably futile and restricts the view of new opportunities. For others, it may be a negative past that they wish they could change. However, to visualize a happier future may require some to give up on wishing for a happier past. Learning from the past does not require reliving it, wishing it were different, or trying to change it. Far more important than what has happened to us in life is how we respond to it.

I am still determined to be cheerful and happy,
in whatever situation I may be; for I have also learned
from experience that the greater part of our happiness or misery
depends upon our dispositions, and not upon our circumstances.
—Martha Washington

Chapter Ten

Highly Rewarded Skills

———————————•———————————

You can have brilliant ideas, but if you can't get
them across, your ideas won't get you anywhere.
—Lee Iacocca

*In looking for opportunities, one talent stands out above all
others as having the greatest potential to influence personal results: communication skills. Since so many people are often weak
in both oral and written communication skills, those who excel in
this arena usually have a marked advantage in life.*

*Effective presentation skills, when developed, give a great re-
turn on investment. With public speaking being such a common
fear, many people avoid situations that require this ability. As a
result, when someone actually stands out in this area, many ob-
servers will associate this skill with leadership potential, and that
person gets more than the usual share of opportunities.*

Relying on Facts

We've all heard the popular expression, "The facts speak for
themselves." However, this is usually wrong. Facts can be

abundant and may appear obvious, but if poorly articulated, they will get few results. In 1929, Dr. Alexander Fleming presented his discovery of penicillin to his peers. Although this drug was a breakthrough in medical science, he was unable to create any enthusiasm or support among his contemporaries. Many believe this failure resulted from his extremely boring delivery style. As a consequence of Fleming's poor presentation, the introduction of this lifesaving drug was delayed for another ten years.

Being unable to get one's ideas across in an effective presentation can be a serious handicap. Learning to convey messages to others successfully is an overriding success factor in most opportunities.

Knowing Your Audience

The most important step in any presentation is to understand the people to whom you will be speaking. The following story strongly emphasizes this point:

> A jealous husband who suspected his wife of being unfaithful called home. The maid answered the phone. The husband said, "Let me speak to my wife, please."
>
> The maid said, "Sir, she's with another man. And I want to let you know that I wholeheartedly disapprove."
>
> He said, "I'll tell you what I want you to do. I want you to go to my desk and get my pistol. Then I want you to walk into the bedroom. Shoot her

- continued -

first, then him, and then report back to the telephone for further instructions."

"Yes, sir," she replied.

He waited a little while and then he heard, "BANG! BANG!" There was more silence. The maid returned to the phone. He asked, "Did you do it?"

"Yes, sir."

"What did you do with the pistol?"

"I threw it in the pool."

"Pool? I don't have a pool! What number is this?"

Knowing who you are talking to is always important! The better the speaker understands the audience, the easier it is to relate to their situation. Also, when you demonstrate this understanding, the audience may warm up or connect to you without even necessarily knowing why.

Watching Your Language

"Watch your language" was a warning I heard constantly as a small child. My mother ground this message into me, and today the advice is still appropriate, but for a different reason. Communication is enhanced when listeners quickly relate to a message. Unfortunately, obscure or unknown words often make this difficult. Effective communicators speak to people using words the audience understands, not words that are intended to impress rather than communicate. I like to ask people, "How do you feel when someone uses a word you don't understand?"

"I feel stupid."

"Okay, and how do you feel toward somebody who makes

you feel stupid?"

"I don't like 'em."

If you really must use big words or technical jargon, make sure the people you are speaking with understand what you are talking about. When you use a word they do not know, they will just look at you and think, *Who is he trying to impress?* When people do not understand your words, you have a problem.

One of the most common problems in today's business environment is the use of acronyms and initials. The problem is that acronyms and initials often mean different things to different people. The same shortened forms, used in different environments, can mean totally different things.

When I was in Vietnam, there was a lieutenant who had been with a Special Forces unit that managed refugees. The activity was called "civil affairs," and was referred to simply as "CAs." This lieutenant's unit was disbanded, and he was assigned to a pool of people available for other jobs. When he interviewed with our colonel, he was asked if he had any experience with "CAs." He said, "Yes, one or two a week."

The colonel said, "Great! You'll fit in well with our unit." The lieutenant did not understand until later that "CAs" for us did not stand for "civil affairs," but for "combat assaults." This soldier found himself in a radically different assignment thanks to a mutual misunderstanding of "CAs."

While it is okay to use acronyms and initials in conversation, be certain to explain them first so that your listeners understand your intended meaning. The difference between the two interpretations of "CAs" could not have been greater.

The ability to understand often requires learning a culture, which often has its own terminology. In the Army, learning to communicate required learning the Army's special alphabet words—"alpha," "bravo," "charlie," and so on—along with other radio protocols. I felt comfortable with the basics of Army communications when I arrived in Vietnam. However, when I joined my company and listened to a radio transmission between two soldiers, I knew I had a problem. Immediately, I became aware of a new language. I heard, "Call me back on the romeo if you find any tangos running off that hotel, and I'll put a Wilson Picket on the deck." I thought, *I expected a learning curve, but this is ridiculous.* I had absolutely no idea what they were talking about. I quickly asked for an explanation and was told it meant they should call back on the radio if they found any trails running off the hill, and we would put a white phosphorous artillery round on the ground.

Every organization has its own special language that may not be official or even widely known. The phrase "he speaks our language" has always been a compliment. Using your audience's language helps demonstrate your knowledge of who they are and their situation.

Pausing for Power

The most notable difference between an amateur speaker and a professional often comes down to pauses. Well-placed pauses, with careful attention to pace and inflection, can turn a mediocre presentation into one that is persuasive and engaging.

Often speakers worry that they will talk too fast, and as a result they present their ideas too slowly. The average person can process between 800 and 1,200 words per minute, but only speaks between 125 and 175 words per minute. So no matter how fast someone speaks, we will have ample time to listen and to understand. In fact, there is so much time that we can even take little mental vacations. And when someone speaks very slowly, we tend to take *lots* of those little mental vacations—and sometimes we never come back.

For example, I speak between 175 and 200 words a minute, with occasional gusts of up to 300 words per minute! Even then people take their little mental side trips. Sometimes it is better to pick up the pace, so that people have less time for other thoughts. You might ask, "Can't you speak *too* fast?" You certainly can. In that case, add more pauses. Years ago, on a FedEx commercial, the actor spoke 600 words a minute. He spoke so rapidly, I couldn't follow everything he said. I could keep up with him for awhile, but then I would get tired and just tune him out completely. If he had paused once or twice, I would have caught up with him and stayed tuned in to his message.

Pausing has other advantages, too. My mother once told me a story about pauses—it's one of my favorites. When she was a high school teacher, one of her extracurricular assignments was to conduct a speech contest at the county fair. Participating students would get five points of extra credit. One year, a young man named Harvey signed up for the competition. He was failing my mother's class, though not by much. He really needed those extra five points.

As you might imagine, Harvey was not a very good speaker. During practice, he kept forgetting his lines and looking all around—at the floor, at the audience, at the ceiling. My mother told him, "When you forget your lines, just look out to the audience, and pause until it comes to you. Then continue with the presentation." Pauses, according to my mother, not only allow us to remember our lines, but also add drama to what we are saying. The night of the contest came. Harvey forgot his lines so frequently, and paused so much, that the judges thought he was the most dramatic speaker of the bunch. He won the contest!

Talkers have always ruled. They will continue to rule. The smart thing is to join them.
—Congressman Bruce Barton

Eyeing Results

Of all presentation skills, eye contact is possibly the most essential for making a strong impact and connecting with the audience. I often ask my audiences, "What do you think of someone who will not look you in the eye?" The answers are unanimously negative:

"That shows he's lying."

"She has poor self-esteem."

"He isn't interested in what I'm saying."

Americans tend to dislike people who will not look them in the eye. When talking to a group of people, try to look at each person in the audience at some point. Eye contact is even more important in one-on-one interactions. When we fail to look directly at someone, we run the risk of offending them.

Keep in mind that there are cultures in which looking people in the eye is a form of disrespect. The rule that applies is to follow the customs of the country where you are at the time. People visiting the United States from other countries usually notice that most Americans look people in the eye, unless they are lying or have poor self-esteem.

I have found that in some situations people look away when you look at them. During my presentations, I have noticed some people who will allow someone to look at them for no more than two seconds. If you look at them for three seconds, they break eye contact. I asked my psychiatrist friend, Dr. Stephen Preas, "What makes people do this?"

He said, "It's the intensity. They can't handle that degree of intensity, whatever the reason."

I try to keep people from becoming uncomfortable during my presentations. If I see that someone is a two-second person, I look at them for a second and a half and then look away, to keep them from having to break eye contact. Many people only look at the person they are talking to for about one second. Generally, that shows a lack of confidence. When you hold eye contact for a longer period of time, the person begins to feel, "He's talking to me."

While training new instructors for AT&T's National Sales School, my colleagues and I knew that the instructors teaching sales skills would have to "practice what they preached" about the crucial role of eye contact. We used a powerful exercise to help the instructors master this skill. It was called the "shooting-down-the-hands" drill. Each presenter was required to stand in front of the class and talk on a subject. All audience members sat with one hand raised. The hand went down when that audience member received five seconds of uninterrupted eye contact. The audience member, counting silently, determined the five-second threshold: one thousand one, one thousand two . . . If at any point the speaker glanced away, the count began again when eye contact was reestablished. All the hands needed to be "shot down" before the speaker could conclude. For some, it took fifteen minutes to shoot down ten hands. In debriefing after the activity, we pointed out that five seconds is a lot longer than most people realize, and that much time is not always required. The exercise, however, dramatically illustrated how frequently presenters fail to maintain eye contact longer than one to two seconds.

In most cases, you want to look for three to five seconds at the person you are speaking to. That is the amount of time it takes for them to feel that you are talking *with* them as opposed to talking *at* them. In one-on-one conversation, it is polite for the speaker to look away periodically. It isn't a contest to see who can stare the longest without looking away. And here is the good news: the person talking is the one whose role it is to look away. The person doing the listening is free and safe to look at the speaker the entire time and to break eye contact at any time.

Upon concluding a presentation to a group of a hundred participants, a woman approached offering positive and enthusiastic feedback. She said, "It seemed like you were speaking to each one of us individually."

She was not aware that she was complimenting me for my eye contact with that group, but that is exactly what it was. That "shoot-down-the-hands" training was the minor opportunity that prepared me for the major opportunities in my profession.

Projecting Confidence

A speaker's comfort level and confidence are often conveyed through gestures and movement. Many people have heard, "If your hands were tied

> **People who feel good about themselves take up more space and convey greater confidence.**

behind your back, you would not be able to talk." Comments such as this have misled many to avoid gesturing. It is not only natural to talk with your hands, but it is an important part of a normal communication process. People often look strange when they stand in front of an audience and continuously hold their hands down, frozen by their sides. This is the "I am going to give an official presentation" look. In seeking to look professional, they often look stiff and unnatural. Gestures are so common that people can often be seen gesturing while driving and talking on their cellular phones.

Psychologists say that the broader and more expansive your gestures, the more confidence you convey. If you want broader gestures, get your arms out from the trunk of your body. In contrast, people who do not feel good about themselves or their message will take up a minimal amount of space. They often stand in one spot and do not move. What they communicate is, "I have this little message; then I'll leave and I won't bother anybody." People who feel good about themselves take up more space and convey greater confidence. Can you gesture too much? Yes, you can. You do not want to look as if you are fighting bees. At the same time, I find that when people err, they err on the side of not gesturing enough. A key to remember is that the audience is not consciously noticing every gesture. If you inadvertently scratch your itching arm during a presentation, most people will not even notice. The danger comes with repetition. If you unconsciously scratch your arm multiple times, then people begin to wonder if you have some kind of problem. The idea is to avoid doing anything that distracts from the content of your message. Gestures should always enhance your message.

Showing Expression

Before you utter a word, you have already begun to deliver a message that, although silent, speaks volumes. That is the message borne out by the expression on your face. If you do not think you communicate with the expression on your face, think about being at a party with your significant other. From the other side of the room, and with just one look, a message can be conveyed letting you know that you are in trouble. No words are spoken, but the message can come across loud and clear.

Your facial expression should match your message. You would not walk into a room with a big smile on your face and say, "Hey! Guess who died?" Of course, you need to know your situation, but smiling is important and best used frequently in appropriate situations. There is no better way to spark a positive response from people than by smiling. When you are talking about a depressing subject, how in the world do you smile? It can be done.

> **Before you utter a word, you have already begun to deliver a message, that although silent, speaks volumes.**

Here is how one woman, a friend of mine, masterfully handles a serious subject, but still finds a way to smile. She often speaks on the subject of child abuse. It is a subject that does not exactly lend itself to smiling. She always starts by talking about the joys of parenting, which affords her the opportunity to smile. She knows the danger of giving an entire presentation without smiling. She starts with a subject she can smile about and then adjusts her expressions when she changes to more serious topics.

A problem often arises when people are more concerned about their success than their message. This concern is often broadcasted in their facial expressions—expressions of doubt, fear, and lack of self-confidence. But if you want to connect with people and be more self-confident at the same time, begin with a little thing that will help move the rest of your body; simply smile.

We shall never know all the good that
a simple smile can do.
—Mother Teresa of Calcutta

Bonding Quickly

Professional speakers are acutely aware of the need to bond with their audience. Most try to arrive early enough before the speech to meet people, introduce themselves, and physically shake as many hands as possible. Connecting early gives them opportunities to make a positive impression on the audience.

A woman in one of my classes related her experience as an attendee at a public seminar. She said the day was to start at 8:30 with coffee and doughnuts, and the class was scheduled to begin at 9:00. She arrived at 8:35 and was the only person there except for another woman, seated in a front corner, drinking coffee and reading. By 9:00, all participants were in their seats and ready to begin. At this point the woman in the corner stood, walked to the center of the room, and started her seminar.

I asked my class for their opinion of this presenter. Their answers were that she was cold, uncaring, self-centered, and did not want to work unless she was being paid. But the most likely reason for her lack of early interaction was that she was going over her notes in order to perform at her best. However, that was not the perception she created with her actions.

I saw this same missed opportunity with salespeople who invited clients to our executive briefing center for presentations.

The presentation would be scheduled for 9:00, and the salespeople would often arrive about 8:15 to give final touches to slide preparations and room arrangements. This became a problem when clients also arrived early. Because unpredictable street traffic prevented our clients from knowing how long their drive might take, sometimes they would allow extra time for their trips and would arrive forty-five minutes early. The salespeople, having come early to prepare for their presentations, would often ignore their clients. My point to them was always the same: if you are working on your slides and materials while the client is there, the subtle message is that your presentation is more important than your client. If instead you immediately focus all your attention on the client, the message is that the client is more important. I always stressed the need to prepare ahead of time and never to use the hour before a client's scheduled arrival time for anything other than communicating and bonding with those clients.

Setting Up for Success

Room setup also plays a role in communication dynamics. If interaction among participants is desired, the chairs should be positioned so that each person can see the maximum number of eyes. I am always amazed when group discussion is desired and the room is set up in a classroom layout. The traditional school classroom setup was designed for teachers to have maximum control, with the students only responding to the teacher and with interaction among pupils being discouraged. (Remember, "No talking to your neighbors!") The reason a classroom setup is less effective for interaction than a horseshoe or roundtable arrangement is that the members cannot see everyone, and constantly turning one's neck becomes extremely uncomfortable. Thus, communication between participants is naturally discouraged or even eliminated altogether.

I remember arriving in Louisville, Kentucky, on the night before a keynote presentation. Although the hour was late, I decided to drop by the banquet room to check out the room setup. To my surprise, I found the top executive from my client company in the room, rearranging the setup to make sure the smallest details were perfect for her presentation. Her attention to detail played a major role in her success.

Writing to Win

Today there is a growing weakness in written communication skills. Even many college-educated employees are deficient in effective business writing skills. This weakness is being exposed like never before with the sudden dramatic growth of the use of e-mails in today's business environment. E-mails speed up communication and cause everyone to respond much more quickly than in the past—and sometimes without as much time for thought. Organizations, in seeking to reduce expenses, have reduced administrative support.

Verbal and grammatical mistakes, while not always obvious on the phone, can become glaring in e-mails.

Most managers now type their own correspondence, without the benefit of any administrative "polishing." Verbal and grammatical mistakes, while not always obvious on the phone, can become glaring in e-mails, thus diminishing one's professional image. This prevalent weakness in written communication skills provides an example of how even the most routine task should be viewed as an opportunity.

I recently discovered a unique tactic that forces individuals to demonstrate their written communications skills on the spot in order to succeed in a formal job interview opportunity. While working with a client, I noticed he had an unusually strong organization. When I asked him some questions about his management practices and hiring procedures, he revealed a unique interviewing tactic, which had played a key role in his success in building a talented team.

At the conclusion of interviews with potential salespeople, he hands candidates a legal pad and pencil. He asks the applicants to take a few minutes before leaving and summarize the interview, then drop the summary off with his secretary on the way out.

He explained that he started using this approach after finding that many people who seemed very skilled in their oral answers to interview questions were inadequate in written communications skills. He acknowledged that applicants have many times honed and perfected their verbal responses through multiple interviews. These apparently skilled applicants did not always work out very well, though, and many later struggled in writing effective business proposals. Although my client had previously designed unique questions to further challenge job candidates, he wanted a method that tested the applicant in a different way. This "summarizing" approach gave him additional insights into the skill sets of the applicants, because any deficiency in written communications skills became immediately apparent in the written summaries.

My client discovered that this technique allowed candidates to demonstrate their ability to quickly analyze and organize relevant points and opportunities. He looked for quality in the writing. He wanted to see persuasiveness and conciseness in their summaries. Creativity also played an important role in his evaluation. His favorite summary simply read, "This is the best candidate that we have interviewed yet. We should hire him immediately." He explained that they did hire the candidate who wrote that summary, and he proved to be very successful and an asset to the company. This was the first applicant who had approached the written summary from the interviewer's perspective.

While the fundamentals of communications seldom change, the vehicle of expression often does. Identifying the corresponding pitfalls of the changing communication media will always present new opportunities for those who are alert.

I have always felt that my ability to deliver an effective presentation early in my career played a tremendous role in the opportunities that came to me. It is also important to remember that one does not need to be in corporate America to reap great benefits from developing these skills. It is a skill that nearly everyone can learn, and it should be recognized as an opportunity generator.

Opportunities multiply as they are seized.
—Sun Tzu

Chapter Eleven

Successful Politics

———————————•———————————

Turn on to politics, or politics will turn on you.
—Ralph Nader

Individuals in today's organizations have many opportunities to make corporate politics work for them. While some use politics to their advantage, others cringe at the thought of involving themselves in anything political—just hearing the term "politics" is a big turnoff. However, politics is a fact of life in every organization.

Fundamentally, corporate politics is neither good nor bad; it is simply a part of every environment to some degree, whether we like it or not. You can choose to do something to increase your influence in your organization's political landscape, or you can ignore it. Whatever you choose to do, though, politics will still have an impact on your opportunities, your career, and ultimately, your life.

———————————•———————————

Addressing Reality

Many people believe that large companies are more politcal than small companies. But in reality, small-company politics often can be far deadlier. For instance, if you have not married the son or daughter of the boss, your opportunity to move to the top may be completely out of the question.

Politics will always be with us. You cannot issue an order, declare a prohibition, or do anything else to drive politics out of existence. You might say, "I'm not political! I don't want to play those games. I just want to do my job and get my just rewards." You are not alone in feeling that way. As an example, here is what often takes place in career-planning workshops:

A group of employees is directed to attend a two-day workshop on career planning. Most of the attendees do not seem to think there is anything wrong with the way they have planned their careers. Others think there is no need to plan their careers. In fact, they say their careers would be going perfectly well if it were not for all the politics. They sit with their arms crossed. Their faces say it all: "I don't want to be here discussing this stupid stuff." The instructor smiles, looks at them, and says, "Take out a sheet of paper. I want everyone to answer this question: 'What is it that drives you crazy in this organization [or company]?'" That gets their attention. A collective groan often comes from the class. Some will even exclaim, "I don't have enough paper!"

When they are finished, some people have written a full page. They are pleased to share their answers with everyone. The instructor writes their comments on the easel. The answers are typically the same: politics, lack of direction from upper management, bureaucracy, and red tape.

The instructor then asks, "Is that it?"

Someone will say, "Yep. Now, what are *you* going to do about it?"

"It's a fair question. Ladies and gentlemen, there is nothing we're going to do in these two days that is going to change any of this. This is the environment in which we live and work. The question is, 'What can we do to better manage our careers?' What you see here is, 'Welcome to corporate America.' You can leave here and go to any major company in the United States; we can have the same career-planning session and ask the same question. The answers will be the same. These are the basic complaints, with politics almost always heading the list."

One of the penalties for refusing to
participate in politics is that you end up
being governed by your inferiors.
—Plato

Why She Was Chosen

In one of my past corporate jobs, five district marketing managers were in my group. Every time a promotional opportunity came up, these five managers would get together to consider the candidates. Each manager would bring the name of a candidate for recommendation. After discussing each name, they decided who would get the promotion. Do you think the best candidate always got the promotion? Think again.

Let's say Mary Lou was the sharpest, most talented

individual in the pool of candidates but was not well known. Mildred was not as talented; however, every single district manager at that meeting knew Mildred. Which of those two got the promotion?" In most cases, Mildred did.

> **The known is often advantaged over the unknown, even though the unknown may in fact be more qualified.**

It may not seem fair, but when the names are presented, it is assumed that every candidate is qualified for the job, or the manager would not be advocating the candidate. This assumption may or may not be correct, but the assumption is made and accepted. Now, assuming that all the people are qualified, familiarity becomes a major variable. The known is often advantaged over the unknown, even though the unknown may appear, and may in fact, be more qualified.

Let me give you an analogy of choosing airlines for travel. I ask audiences, "What is the most important variable in flying?"

They answer, "Safety! I don't want to crash!"

I respond with "I agree; however, when you book a flight with an airline, you look at two primary factors: cost and scheduling. Maybe you consider whether you want frequent-flier miles, but not much else figures in. Safety is not your number one selection criterion. You assume that all planes will be safe. It may not be true, but it is your assumption, and you will have to live—or die—with your decision.

When it comes to a promotion, it often works in much the same way—the assumption is that everyone on the promotion list is qualified. If everyone is qualified, then it comes down to who is best known in a positive light. Who is it that most people know well enough to have developed a positive opinion about them? As has been discussed earlier, those who are perceived in a positive light have made the most of their minor opportunities. That positions them favorably for this major (promotion) opportunity. This is how many decisions are made, like it or not. It is part of corporate politics.

But Do They Know You

There was a time in my career when I worked in a division of the company located far from the corporate office and its leadership. My facility was not exactly a hotbed of activity. It was a rare occasion when we would actually see a top executive, which also meant that it was a rare occasion when an executive would get to see us. It seemed the only time we actually saw an executive was at a retirement or promotion party. When the executives would ask us to attend a party, a lot of people would say, "I'm not going to any party! It's after five o'clock. I'm going home. I'm not hanging around just because some executive is in town." I thought to myself, *It is certainly your right not to stay beyond five o'clock. But isn't it foolish?* It would always amaze me when people did not take advantage of those opportunities to become known by those with the power to advance their careers.

Just doing your job may get you a regular paycheck. "Just doing the job" is the minimum that is expected. However, doing the minimum is not going to make you stand out as exceptional. People are not going to get to know you. Remember, when you look at the variables for career advancement, a primary one is being well known and highly perceived. And you must be known before you can be highly perceived.

For example, let's say Fred and I develop a method for making cheap cups. I already have a full-time job, and so does Fred. We have a way to produce these cups, but we need somebody to sell them. Are we going to put an ad in the newspaper looking for the world's best cup salesman? I doubt it. I am going to say, "Fred, I have a friend who would do a great job for us." We would hire the friend because we know her. That is the way the world often works, and that is the way promotions work, particularly in large organizations. In any decision, people seek to minimize the unknown factors because these represent risks. For decision makers, the more they know, the less risk they feel. Generally, jobs are awarded to someone the decision makers know. They may not be hiring the best person, but they do not know the other applicants as well and are usually more willing to place their bet on the known.

Simply doing your job well or even better than everyone else does not automatically qualify you for a promotion. The fact that you have done your job is expected, but achieving some minimal level of performance seldom prompts a promotion. There must be other variables.

It's all the same thing: politics, "the good ol' boy network"—networking.

"Oh, it's politics," you might say, or "It's the 'good ol' boy' network." Or you might tell me, "It's not *what* you know, it's *who* you know. It's not fair."

These are typical comments. However, people express a very different perspective when asked about networking. "Oh, networking is great," they say. "It gives you a chance to meet people who can help you get ahead." It's all the same thing: politics, "the good ol' boy network"—networking. There is no difference. It is all about getting to know people, about bonding, about developing and maintaining relationships to help further your career possibilities. Networking will position you to take advantage of opportunities that arise. By failing to network, you will likely ensure that you are not even around to be thought of or identified, and thus will not be given the opportunities that abound. Failing to network will likely keep you right where you are, doing whatever you do, for a long time.

Higher profiles usually translate to greater opportunities.

Some people enhance their exposure by using the media, both internal and external. For example, being featured in a company periodical for a major accomplishment can certainly make a difference. Higher profiles usually translate to greater opportunities.

Reputations That Precede Us

When I ask people, "Do you think people are influenced by reputation?" they reply, "Oh, yes!" When I ask, "What goes into somebody's reputation?" I get those old, standard replies about superficial, political considerations: "Well, people get ahead who only say what management wants to hear, who dress like management, who spend all their time getting to know everybody."

I then like to ask, does dependability play a role? If you give somebody certain work to do and they mess it up, do you always keep it quiet? Or might you later say, "If you give that to Marvin, he's going to mess it up. You can count on it; he has a problem every time." Do you think that would have an impact on Marvin's reputation? Certainly, it does. Also, consider Shirley who is good at what she does. Every time you give her a project, it is done, hassle free. You know that when she tells you she's going to do it, you can count on it, on time and without mistakes. In this example, Marvin failed to turn his situational opportunities into situational success while Shirley succeeded. Does that contribute to her reputation? Again, yes. Would your decision on whom to use for a project be influenced by these examples? Would your decision to promote someone be influenced by these same examples? Absolutely!

Those who recognize and take advantage of the opportunities to provide more value find more success.

A good reputation is essential to facilitate the number and quality of opportunities as well as the success rate of those opportunities. Without a good reputation, you may never get the opportunities to prove yourself further and enjoy success. The variables that determine reputation are built from many situations, both minor and major.

What Are You Worth

Many times organizations perceive value differently from the way individual team members do. I believe the following story accurately describes the potential difference in valuation.

A young fellow about nine years old applied for a job to sack groceries at a small neighborhood grocery store for his first summer job. Though the grocer had known the boy for most of his life, he humored the youngster by simulating an interview. The grocer asked, "Well, Billy, how much experience do you have?"

Billy promptly replied, "None."

The grocer then asked, "Well, with no experience, how much money would you want to sack groceries?"

- continued -

Again Billy spoke right up: "Ten dollars an hour."

Taken aback, the grocer asked, "Why so much?"

The prompt reply was, "Why, sir, when you don't know what you're doing, the work is much harder."

Some people believe their value should be based on how hard they work. And while effort and hard work are certainly important factors, other variables, such as education, experience, and meaningful contribution, will almost always be considered in how a team member is valued. Those who recognize and take advantage of the opportunities to provide more value typically find more success.

People will sit up and take notice of you,
if you will sit up and take notice of what
makes them sit up and take notice.
—Frank Romer

We should always remain vigilant to ways we can add more value to what we do. Several years ago, I made a presentation in Myrtle Beach, South Carolina. I finished my speech at nine in the morning, and my flight back to Atlanta was not until five that afternoon. I said to myself, *I have some extra time; I think I'll go soak up some sun.* So I put on my bathing suit and went out to the pool. In no time at all, my lily-white skin began to burn. I realized I needed something to fix the problem or I was going to be in trouble. I looked up from my lounge chair and saw a sign on the other side of the pool that read, "Suntan Consultant." Now, I had heard of these people, but I had never actually met one. There was an attractive young woman in a bikini, selling suntan lotion. I raised my hand and said, "I have the need right here." When she came over, I told her, "I'm not going to be here long, and I want the smallest tube of lotion you have." She handed me a tube about two inches long.

"That will be $7.50," she said.

My eyes bulged as I thought, *$7.50? Whew!* I felt totally ripped off. I felt as if I were at a professional sporting event trying to buy a hot dog. But what I did not understand was the "added value" that was included in that $7.50. She not only put the suntan lotion on me, she came back and told me when to turn so she could put it on the other side. That was the best $7.50 I ever spent in my life!

Always do more than is required of you.
—General George S. Patton

Perceptions That Matter

Bill worked for me several years ago. He was a good employee, a hard worker, and one of my top salespeople. He always gave me his best. However, he lived about sixty miles from the office. A sixty-mile ride in the Atlanta area on the weekend might take about an hour. But during the weekday rush hour, that same ride could take more than twice as long. To avoid the traffic on his long commute to the office, Bill would come in early, arriving at work every day around seven o'clock in the morning. He was a family man who liked to leave a little before five o'clock to beat the traffic. The earlier he left, the more time he could spend with his wife and kids in the evening. That was fine with me, but not with my boss. My boss was not a man who started work early. He got in about nine o'clock and stayed late. He was the kind who, at the end of the day, would sort of "cruise" the building (often referred to as MBWA—management by walking around.) He would move from office to office and chat with employees.

I covered for Bill as best I could when the boss would ask, "Where's Bill?"

I would explain, "He comes in early and goes home early. It gives him a jump on the traffic." One day Bill and I were working on a major project. The project was so big that our headquarters in New Jersey was involved. It was a $6 million sales opportunity, and we were waiting for some information in order to complete our special bid. The special-bids group called my boss about five o'clock and asked a question that only Bill could answer. My boss came to my office, looking for Bill.

"Where's Bill?" he asked.

"You just missed him. He just walked out," I said.

My boss turned and walked off mumbling, "I have never in my life seen a salesperson worth a damn who leaves work at five o'clock!"

The next morning I called Bill into my office. "Bill," I said, "Let me tell you something. You have expressed to me a desire to get promoted, but I see a problem. I don't have any problem with your work, with the contribution you make, with your results or your success rate. You do a good job for me, and I will continue to give you a hundred percent support for what you do. However, my boss does have a problem with the hours you keep. He doesn't feel you are properly dedicated, as evidenced by your leaving at or before five o'clock. It just flies in the face of what he believes. I'm not saying he's right; I'm just telling you what the politics in this situation are. If you want to get promoted, I suggest you figure out some way that you can be here after five o'clock. That's the time when he comes by, checks, and has his conversations with people. I'm not telling you what to do. I'm just 'putting a bug in your ear' to help you meet your career objectives."

Perceptions are seldom changed with words, but rather with demonstrated behaviors.

Shortly thereafter, Bill sold his house and bought a house about ten miles from the office. He was soon promoted. A lot of people would say, "I'm not doing that! My hours are my hours." That is your business, of course; however, you must understand the realities and likely consequences of your decisions. For the most part, you do not want your boss coming in before you or leaving after you.

The most important "takeaway" from this example is that perception is reality. My job at that time was to try to alter my boss's perception of Bill. Bill (to fulfill his desire to get promoted) had to give me something to work with. Perceptions are seldom changed with words, but rather with demonstrated behaviors. Do not complain and grumble about the perceptions people have of you. Work on changing those perceptions through your actions. Some may refer to that sort of activity as "politics." I prefer to think of it as taking control of your future. I believe that positive perceptions position you for success. For Bill, opportunity existed, and he used it to achieve success.

There Are Stupid Questions

To some degree our reputation is formed from the collective interactions we have with all the other members of a group. When we ask a great question, our reputation can move upward, while an inopportune question can have the opposite effect. The old saying "there is no such thing as a stupid question" is, well, stupid. My son taught me this when he was only five years old and had just learned to ride his bike. He pulled out of our driveway, lost his balance, and fell. He was lying in the street with his bike half on top of him, trying to decide whether to cry. I was standing in the yard and had seen his accident, so I yelled to him, "Kenny, are you all right?"

> I was interviewing a young woman for a sales position and asked her what she saw as her greatest weakness. She paused for a second and said, "Laziness." I thought to myself, *Nope, poor judgment.*

He looked back over his shoulder at me and screamed, "Does someone lying in the street like this *look* like they are all right?!" Obviously, my question was rather stupid.

Yes, we do get evaluated both on our questions and on our answers. People do form opinions based on both what we say and what we do. Reputations can form quickly and are often hard to change. I was interviewing a young woman for a sales position and asked her what she saw as her greatest weakness. She paused for a second and said, "Laziness." I thought to myself, *Nope, poor judgment.* Her answer to that one question sealed her fate in the interview. Nothing else she could have said would have erased that firmly entrenched perception of "lazy" from my mind.

You can tell whether a man is clever by his answers.
You can tell whether a man is smart by his questions.
—Naguib Mahfouz,
Nobel Prize Winner in Literature

What Goes Around . . .

Do you remember the Dr. Seuss story *Yertle the Turtle*? In this delightful fantasy, Yertle is king of the pond. Yertle believes he rules all that he can see. The turtles pile themselves higher and higher to allow Yertle to see more. Yertle is dethroned, however, due to a single turtle. As Dr. Seuss put it, "His burp shook the throne of a king!" Yertle the Turtle, king of all that he saw, came tumbling down.

Those who climb the ladder of success by taking advantage of their peers and their teams do not earn respect from the people they climb over. They may use their power to instill fear, but they are not gaining the respect and trust they will need to be successful in the long term.

When you ride to the top on other people's backs, the people at the bottom know what is happening. They know that you, like Yertle, cannot do it without them. They also know when you are not showing them appreciation and when you are taking credit for the things they have done. They will not be happy and will become cynical. They will find ways to let you know they are around, even if they have to let out "one heck of a burp" to do so!

I believe in the old adage "What goes around comes around." When someone steps on people to get ahead, the benefits reaped are generally only for the short term. It looks good for a while, but don't turn your back. You may find yourself in the position of needing to depend on those same people to get you out of the proverbial ditch. You could be creating a network of people who are looking for an opportunity to take a shot at you. And when they shoot, they will most likely hit you in a place where it will hurt a lot. There is no reason to make enemies when you do not have to.

While seeking upward mobility in any organization, it is best to build relationships with the people you will need to get you there. You want to be able to count on them on your road to the top. It might take a little bit longer and require a bit more effort, but that foundation is required for long-term success. You may have to be nice to some people you do not particularly like. But because

You are best positioned for further success by building respect among your peers and your managers.

you have secured a foundation based on mutual respect, people are more pleased with your success and are more willing to help you achieve your goals. At minimum, your colleagues will more likely be neutral and not work to your detriment. The broader-based your network of support, the more likely your career successes.

Make sure that you do not start networking upward and "politicking" to the neglect of those at your level. The influence of your peers is enormous. If you do not have their respect, they may make comments about you behind your back that can damage your career forever. You want to be known as somebody who does his or her share of the work and is likable, dependable, and professional. Develop those connections; *then* start moving up. Someday you may be leading these people, and then you will really need their respect. You are best positioned for further success by building respect among your peers and your managers.

Fear of appearing phony or self-serving keeps many individuals from even attempting higher-level relationships. While no one likes phony people, nearly everyone at every level likes having friends. We enjoy having relationships with other people. There is nothing wrong with spending time with people who can help you. It is essential if you want to get ahead. That is why it is difficult to work only from eight to five. If you're working eight to five and nothing beyond that, yet you are doing your politicking in the boss's office during those hours, you are setting yourself up for criticism. Schmooze on your own time, not on the company's, and not while your peers are working hard and resenting your schmoozing.

All Things Being Equal

Earlier I wrote about being located in an office away from the center of power. There are a lot of advantages to being so located—you do not have to look over your shoulder, and you often have more autonomy. Sometimes you can dress more casually than they do at headquarters. But I always preferred being located at headquarters; it is usually the place to be if you want to get ahead. In most cases, you automatically have access to more potential opportunities. When you call an executive on the phone from a remote location, he or she is expecting a purpose for your call—there must be some kind of agenda. If you are in the same building, you can often walk into that executive's office without an agenda and informally talk or share an idea.

Being with people when you do not need them or have to be with them creates a different dynamic. If you call somebody only when you need something from him or her, there always has to be an agenda; it will never be an informal conversation. Thus, your chances of building or sustaining a relationship are limited. But if you can call somebody when you do not need anything, a stronger bond will frequently result.

All things being equal, people prefer doing business with friends; all things being unequal, people still prefer doing business with friends.

You will move the relationship more toward that of a friend. You have the option to talk about work, the weather, the world, last night's ballgame, or anything else. It is in these informal conversations that you begin to understand other people's values, how they think and judge what is important to them. It also allows them to gain the same understanding about you. This is why networking is so effective.

By interacting in this way, without an agenda, you begin to influence others' opinion of you and your ideas, and to give them a comfort level with how you think. You become the kind of person of whom it is said, "I trust him," or "I will move her up (in the organization)." So much of this trust becomes intuitive when you develop that kind of connection. When your manager recommends you for that promotion and somebody says, "Why do you feel this way?" he or she is apt to answer, "I feel good about her judgment," or "I like the way he interacts with people." By having these informal conversations, you create untold opportunities to influence others' opinions in a positive way.

Relationship building has other benefits, too. Through these informal conversations, mentoring relationships can take root, providing you with a sounding board, regardless of your current job and employer. These relationships can last for years or decades.

Most client-focused organizations recognize the importance of fostering relationships with clients, and that is why clients are entertained at baseball games, tennis matches, and other public venues. These informal encounters build trust and allow insights that prove helpful in maintaining relationships. Remember: all things being equal, people prefer doing business with friends; all things being unequal, people still prefer doing business with friends.

Making the "Howdy" Call

A major requirement in making my business work is the ability to have and keep a lot of friends. One relationship that began years before I started my own company proved extremely beneficial years later, when my friend accepted a position with a large company that could possibly use my services. As a result of this single relationship, I was able to generate over a million dollars in speaking engagements from this one client. I was positioned to maximize opportunities I would never have heard about without my friend. This example demonstrates the value of long-standing relationships and how they can pay off, not only in emotional satisfaction, but also monetarily.

One of the ways I maintain my relationships and keep up with my friends and clients is by calling them when I don't need anything. I call these "howdy" calls. I call just to say, "Howdy!" But in order to be able to make a "howdy" call, you need to have an existing relationship. I cannot pick up the phone, call just any random executive at IBM, and say, "Hey, this is Ken Futch. I'm just calling to see how you're doing." She is likely to say, "Who is this idiot, and why is he wasting my time?" You can make "howdy" calls only when you move from being someone who needs something to someone who is a friend. In my business today, I maintain a network of many friends with whom I maintain regular contact through "howdy" calls. I have accumulated this network over many years, and some of the relationships go all the way back to my childhood in Burgaw, North Carolina.

While managing national accounts sales at AT&T, I regularly kept up with most of the people I met at internal meetings and conferences. "Howdy" calls to these people cemented relationships that later proved fruitful when my sales team needed assistance in a distant location. Your goal in building relationships is to move more people into the area where you can make "howdy" calls. It is all part of networking, or organizational politics, and it can prove invaluable down the road.

There is great reward to be found in helping others, and we especially enjoy being able to assist our friends. Turning situational opportunities into success usually involves others, and when friends can help friends achieve success, it is the ultimate win/win.

Those friends thou hast, and their adoption tried,
bind to thyself with hoops of steel.
—William Shakespeare

Chapter Twelve

My Parting Shot

The lure of the distant and the difficult is deceptive.
The great opportunity is where you are.
—John Burroughs

L ife promises no one success, but it provides everyone with opportunities. Our challenge is to improve our recognition of those situational opportunities available to us.

The premise in this book is that we should recognize the minor opportunities in our daily situations, which will provide the foundation for capitalizing on major opportunities in the future.

Success in minor situations prepares us internally and externally for major opportunities. We are able to begin believing in our abilities, and others begin recognizing our potential. Success does breed success.

Developing a habit of selecting an activity and seeking to excel in it can ignite a new world of possibilities. There is a great thrill and much self-fulfillment in fine-tuning a skill.

What you choose is not always as important as that you choose. After your selection, you can then assess your success and determine if it was worth the effort. If so, build on it and repeat the process. Develop the skills you find rewarding.

With repetition as a primary component, your development can be hastened by learning from others. I have shared ideas, techniques, and lessons that I believe will aid in this process and improve your probability of success.

With a society interdependent on each other, I have placed a great emphasis on understanding the power of relationships and how to more effectively communicate with others.

Learn to spot the opportunities that others miss. Change your focus from looking for opportunities that may become available to recognizing the existing opportunities that are currently available. Remember, opportunities are often not obvious and nearly always require development.

Start where you are. Begin the cycle of success. Turn your situational opportunities into situational successes. Choose your opportunity and *take your best shot.*

Destiny is not a matter of chance;
it is a matter of choice.
It is not a thing to be waited for,
it is a thing to be achieved.
—William Jennings Bryan

Epilogue

———————————•———————————

I always tried to turn every
disaster into an opportunity.
—John D. Rockefeller

In 2002, my son Kenny decided to join the army. Upon completing his training, he was assigned to the 82nd Airborne Division, and within days he was sent to serve in Afghanistan. Only months after his return, he again received orders for another combat zone. Knowing he was scheduled to leave for Iraq on January 16, 2004, I was delighted when he called three days before his departure, on his birthday. I immediately began singing happy birthday, which, due to my natural lack of singing talent, always makes him laugh. I could tell, however, that his mood was very somber. During our conversation, I found out why. He related what he had just learned about his unit's advance group. This small group, which had gone to Iraq a few days earlier, had been attacked on their drive in, and several soldiers had been shot.

Later that day, my wife informed me that in her conversation

———————————•———————————

with Kenny, he revealed how nearly everyone seemed to be terrified. I told her that although he hadn't shared that with me, I certainly understood why anyone would be scared.

The next day he called again. This time he was in a dramatically different mood. He no longer seemed at all concerned about his upcoming departure. He was buoyant and upbeat as he talked about his last-minute preparations. I listened attentively as I pondered the reason for his new attitude.

Without any prompting he said, "Daddy, my first sergeant is in the wrong business. He ought to be a motivational speaker like you. First Sergeant Carabello is wasting his time being in the army!"

"Have you heard him give a speech?" I asked.

"Oh, yes!" he answered, "he gave one this morning."

"Well, what did he say?" I inquired.

"He told us he knew that most of us were scared and worried about going over. 'That, however, is the great news!' he said. 'Because that is what is going to bring you all back alive!' He told us that when someone was too comfortable, they weren't as alert, and that's when people got killed. So he was delighted that we were scared, because that meant that we would all be coming home alive!"

Kenny then said, "Daddy, I would follow that man anywhere. I look at him like my second father."

I thought to myself, *No, that man is not in the wrong business. He's right where he needs to be. We're lucky to have leaders like that serving our country. If my son has to go to war, how wonderful it is that he is serving with someone he respects.*

This is a prime example of someone taking a negative—in this case, fear—and turning it into a positive. My son's sergeant saw the opportunity where others saw only the problem. He enabled his people to see how this negative could in fact be a force for good.

Recognizing and responding to opportunities, particularly in challenging situations, is a learned ability. It can be developed through a combination of perspective, awareness, preparation, and action. By taking better advantage of these everyday opportunities, we can truly enrich our lives and the lives of those around us.

I am opportunity.

I shall pass through this world but once.

Any good that I can show to any human being,

Let me do it now.

Let me not defer nor neglect it,

For I shall not pass this way again.

—adapted from Quaker missionary
Stephen Grellet (1773–1885)

Acknowledgements

———————————•———————————

The completion of this book could not have been accomplished without the encouragement of my family and friends. My wife Linda, my son Kenny, and daughter Karen were a source of inspiration, encouragement and material.

The following friends and clients helped guide my efforts in writing this book and in promoting my career. I owe special thanks for the assistance of:

Carol Hacker • Liz Hall • David Meyers
Gene Griessman • Michael Carr • Gary Trawick
Leslie Rains • Dick Biggs • Larry Kahn
Richard Weylman • Doug Smart • Michael LeBoeuf
Danny Helmly • Lou Heckler • George Langan
Steve Preas • Hal Turner • Judy Futch • Ellen Rusnak
Libby Rooks • David Greenberg • Gentry Dunnagan
Marilynn Mobley • Austin McGonigle • Terry Brock
Toni Boyle • Bob Gibson • Barry Littmann
Jeff Justice • Kate Chestney Spinks • Mark Mayberry
Kevin Machel-Cox • Bill Buehler • Steve Cohn
Don Miller • Janet Richerson • Bill Marianes
Larry Carter • Dan Thurman • Shirley Garrett
Joe Gandolfo • Pam Hammond • Larry Banks

———————————•———————————

Suzan Monk • Bob Peterson • Mike Stewart
Susan Bixler • George Carellas • Chris Carey
Terry Clark • Fred Dees • John Foy • Gail Geary
Tom Giddens • Rod Goelz • Linda Suvalsky
Ralph Reed • Cary Strohecker • Mary Lou Saye
Earle Saye • Dan Maddux • Candy Sherburne
Pete Stycos • Ronnie Thomasson • Benny Williford
Lowell Whitlock • Steve Woodard • Valerie Woodard
Wally Steinhauser • Gene Swindell • Katrina Street
Bill Lampton • Tim Walker • Jim Perry
George Ort • Alf Nucifora • Steve Forrester
Debbie Ballard • Jeanne Sharbuno • Candie Hurley
David Dempsey • Paul Amos • Keith Harrell
Jim Hackbarth • Jim Brinker • Eric Mawyer
Karen Finley • David Perdue • Mike Osredker
Nido Qubein • Brad Walker • Greg Vetter
Terry Snell • Jerry Untiedt • Jay Damiano
Lisa Brinton • Phillip Van Hooser • Susan Savage

Their support provided the ammunition allowing me to take my best shot.

About the Author

●

K en Futch is an internationally recognized speaker, seminar leader, and author with more than 25 years' experience managing and motivating others. He is a graduate of the University of North Carolina at Chapel Hill and was commissioned as a lieutenant and served in Vietnam as a combat platoon leader.

His awards and achievements include the prestigious designation of Certified Speaking Professional (CSP) by the National Speakers Association, and he is a past president of the Georgia Speakers Association. He was recognized at AT&T for being the top revenue producer in a nationwide group of 6,000 salespeople and received the Outstanding Achievement Award for top instructor at the AT&T National Sales School.

Services:

Keynote Presentations

Relevant and customized messages delivered through skillfully crafted inspirational and humorous stories.

Banquets

Hilarious after-dinner entertainment.

Seminars and Workshops

Highly interactive, skills-based programs designed to

Seminars and Workshops (continued)
reinforce learning points through experiential
activities (1/2 day, full day, multiple days).

Personal Success Coaching
Individualized one-on-one coaching designed to
unlock potential, maximize performance, and
accelerate career progression.

Topics:

Motivation
A moment can change a life. Ken's astonishing true
story of how he accidentally shot himself in the
head—and how it opened his mind! Hilarious,
inspiring, and motivating, you will acquire a (w)hole
new perspective on how to turn situations into
opportunities.

Leadership
Gain the single greatest motivation tool available for
creating passion. An entertaining and provocative
program that provides practical principles and
techniques for achieving results.

Customer Service
Move beyond the basics and learn the two
requirements necessary to create memorable
customer-service experiences. Discover how to

Customer Service (continued)

turn that disgruntled customer into a sales opportunity. An upbeat message designed for organizations seeking to increase client retention.

Change

Do you hold on to the old or grab on to the new? Managing change isn't just recognizing the need to change, but knowing how to change. During this humorous and high-energy program, you will acquire the insights and tools to reframe change and to embrace the potential that change offers.

Teamwork

Learn what teams value most while avoiding the common pitfalls that can destroy employee morale. This fast-paced program emphasizes the importance of respecting individuality while enhancing group identity. Take home valuable tools for improving communication and building trust.

Presentation Skills

Empower your message for effective delivery by utilizing the hidden persuaders that enable powerful presentations. Learn to overcome nervousness, organize material, incorporate humor, and handle question-and-answer sessions. Leave with the confidence to connect with demanding audiences.

Sales

Move from commodity-based product selling to value-based benefit selling and differentiate your company from the competition. Build relationships that last long beyond the sales cycle and find that the fortune is in the follow-up. Can your sales force clearly articulate your value proposition? These role-play intensive sessions inject confidence and enthusiasm into your sales teams and give them the motivation to succeed.

For more information and to schedule live appearances, please call, write, fax, or email:

Ken Futch & Associates
2684 Coldwater Canyon Drive
Tucker, Georgia 30084
Phone: 770 939-6200
Fax: 770 270-9929
Email: ken@KenFutch.com
www.KenFutch.com

What Others Are Saying

———————————•———————————

"Rarely have I seen a speaker weave so many different examples into such a humorous yet thought-provoking presentation. Your tale of shooting yourself in the head, complete with actual tabloid coverage, was the piece-de-resistance!"

—Dan Maddux
American Payroll Association

"An audience of bank CEO's can be a tough group. You did a great job of giving them good ideas to take back with them. You are truly a gifted speaker and a funny man."

—Mary Jo Nortrup
Independent Bankers Association of New York

"My life has included a half marathon, half triathlon, 12 years of hockey, 2 years of boxing and some nice vacations, none of which measures up to my two days at your seminar. My new goal in life is to reach someone the way you reached me."

—Jake VanRiper
Guardian Products

"Our sales team was drawn in by your energy and entertained with your humor. Your comments were on target and infused essential sales techniques into the most entertaining illustrations I've ever heard!"

—Cheryl Vowels
Nortel Networks

"When I heard you speak at the Carolinas' Forum for Brick Distributors last year, I thought you were the best motivational speaker in America. Based on your performance this year, I have no reason to change that assessment. You were terrific!"

—Scotty Freebairn
Acme Brick

"You changed our lives by allowing us to learn from your experiences. You were able to expose our audience to not only the facts of life, but also to the key rules to gaining and maintaining success in life. Our investigators left your session with a different outlook on life, work, and family.

Please know that what you do is not motivational speaking. You enrich and change lives."

—McKinley Wooten
Inspector General, State of North Carolina

ORDER FORM

❑ Please send me _____ copies of Take Your Best Shot at $24.95. Add $4.00 for U.S. shipping. Allow 15 days for delivery.

(Call for information on bulk order discounts and Canadian/International shipping.)

❑ My check or money order for $ _____ is enclosed.

❑ Please charge my: ❑ VISA ❑ MasterCard ❑ American Express

Card no. _____

Expiration Date _____

Cardholder _____

Credit Card Billing Address _____

City _____ State _____ Zip _____

Signature _____

❑ Shipping Address

Name _____

Organization _____

Address _____

City _____ State _____ Zip _____

Telephone _____ Fax _____

Email _____

Mail or Fax Order to:

Ken Futch & Associates
2684 Coldwater Canyon Drive
Tucker, Georgia 30084
Phone: 770 939-6200
Fax: 770 270-9929
Email: ken@KenFutch.com
Web: www.KenFutch.com

ORDER FORM

❑ Please send me _____ copies of Take Your Best Shot at $24.95.
Add $4.00 for U.S. shipping. Allow 15 days for delivery.

(Call for information on bulk order discounts and
Canadian/International shipping.)

❑ My check or money order for $ _____ is enclosed.

❑ Please charge my: ❑ VISA ❑ MasterCard ❑ American Express

Card no. _____

Expiration Date _____

Cardholder _____

Credit Card Billing Address_____

City _____ State _____ Zip _____

Signature _____

❑ Shipping Address

Name_____

Organization_____

Address _____

City _____ State _____ Zip _____

Telephone _____ Fax _____

Email _____

Mail or Fax Order to:
   Ken Futch & Associates
   2684 Coldwater Canyon Drive
   Tucker, Georgia 30084
   Phone: 770 939-6200
   Fax: 770 270-9929
   Email: ken@KenFutch.com
   Web: www.KenFutch.com